MAGNETIC MINDSET

HOW TO MAKE LOVE
TO THE UNIVERSE AND
MANIFEST ANYTHING

GALA DARLING

DEDICATION

This book is dedicated to the disco babes, eclectic queens and curious cuties who know that *there is more to life than this.*

May this book open you up to what is possible.

May it allow you to see with new eyes.

May it assist you in experiencing the profound ecstasy of being yourself.

CONTENTS

"Nothing that is happening needs to affect your vibration and therefore needs to affect what is happening to you."—Abraham-Hicks appreciation, and consistency in the gym! I adopted a beautiful dog and met the man of my dreams. And best of all, I wake up every day feeling free, joyful, and excited about what's next.

Listening to Abraham-Hicks unlocked something within me. It reminded me that ecstasy is my birthright, that nothing is outside of the realms of possibility, and that if I want to feel good, I cannot blame anyone else for how I feel. It's all on me.

Within just one year of adopting this new mindset, my life became a vivid example of just how much things can change; how powerful we truly are; and that everything we desire can be made manifest when we approach it the right way. As I continue to practice feeling good, now several years on, it's incredible how much things can bloom and evolve.

These days, I consider the teachings of Abraham-Hicks to be my foundation, and they inform everything else I do. But it is not the only thing I follow or believe in. There are many other beautiful philosophies and tools within this world, and my life has gotten even more delicious when I layer them on top of what I've learned from Abraham.

That's what this book is: an exploration of the various systems that I have used to enhance my life, to make it more beautiful, to make it more easeful. I am going to share with you everything I've discovered about manifesting the life you've always wanted. We will cover everything from creating daily routines to transforming your relationships to clearing your clutter and making your space feel delightful.

I can't wait to jump in. Let's begin. ✳

01

YOU ARE A GODDESS

H AVE YOU EVER HAD ONE OF THOSE DAYS THAT FEELS LIKE a big cosmic joke? Like the Universe is just messing with you? You don't understand what you're doing wrong. Why is nothing working out the way you want it to? Why does life feel so unfair?

Have you ever experienced one of those moments where you lose faith in the Universe? It all seems wrong. It all seems totally hopeless.

Sometimes you don't feel sad—you just feel pissed. You want to grab the Universe and slam its (figurative) head in a car door. You feel so angry and drained and hopeless that you almost can't remember your dreams. You certainly can't comprehend what your life would be like if your dreams came true. It all feels so far away.

Of course you have had those days, because—despite frequent confusion about how the rest of the species are behaving—you are a human being. Being a human is pretty damn good, for the most part. However, for all the fabulousness of being human, we also have some very tricky machinery. Machinery that we don't always understand.

Now, how would you feel if I told you that you are the one creating all this dischord in your life? You might want to throw this book against the wall in a fiery rage, and who could blame you?

I have felt this way many times. I have beaten my head against the wall, wondering whether I was being punished by the Universe in a twist of karmic fate. Maybe I'd done something truly evil in a past life! I've had moments where I have been convinced that it's all terrible. The more I insisted upon how terrible it was, the worse it became. But when I finally get to that point where I pick my face up out of the puddle I am planted in, and make tiny little energetic shifts— say, for example, jotting down daily gratitude lists, or doing EFT/tapping in the mornings—the rest of my life starts to transform too.

The best thing? My life doesn't change because of anything external to me. **It changes because I change my thoughts.**

The reason my thoughts change my life is because we are vibrational beings. That means that it is far more important that we tweak our vibration than anything we might do in the material world.

This might sound abstract, so let me explain it a little bit more. Whatever I focus on, wherever I put my energy and attention, will expand. Have you ever had a real humdinger of a problem? Did you ever notice that when you obsess over and fixate on that problem, it only ever seems to get worse? I have experienced precisely this outcome so many times in so many different areas of my life, from my health to my relationships to my bank balance! Bizarrely, it seems that when I either change my thoughts about the subject—so instead of freaking out over how I don't have enough money, I make an effort to be truly and authentically grateful for what I do have—or I simply stop thinking about the subject as much as possible, the situation changes too. Money shows up. A job comes in. A new client sends an email. Miracles occur!

You already know this from your own life. When you pour love and appreciation into a situation—whether it's being thankful for your friendships or enjoying a creative act—it flourishes. Your pre-existing friendships deepen and you meet new people! When you're enjoying being creative, the work flows. It's easy. You produce some of the best work of your life.

This is a function of both momentum—i.e., putting energy into something allows it to pick up speed, like a snowball, and just get bigger and bigger—and also that our thoughts dictate the conditions of our life.

If you want to approach this from a purely scientific standpoint, you can look at confirmation bias. This is a function of the human brain which means that our beliefs inform our life. With confirmation bias, we are wired to look for things—people, situations, events—that confirm our biases (biases being preconceived notions and prejudices, things we believe to be true about groups of people, or patterns or habits of thinking that we are accustomed to.)

One of the rules of your brain's operating system is that **your subconscious mind will never make you a liar!** In other words, if you believe that all men are dishonest, your subconscious mind will actually go looking for men who prove this to you. In fact, confirmation bias is so powerful that even if you do meet an honest man, you will go looking for instances of his trickiness! (Of course, you will find it, because nobody is completely squeaky clean... And again, your subconscious mind will never make you a liar.)

You can only imagine how our confirmation biases mess with our intimate relationships!

This is not some woo-woo craziness. There are endless scientific experiments which prove that reality is what we make it. (Google "double slit experiment" and "quantum theory reality" if you truly want to geek out.) But if you'd like to bring together the physical (neuroscience, quantum physics and psychology) and the metaphysical, all you need to know is that our thoughts are truly the seedlings of our reality.

If your thoughts create your universe, what does that mean for you, sitting here, reading this?

It means that you are massively powerful. In fact, it means that even when you're sweatpants, hair tied, chilling with no make-up on (as Drake would say)... You are a goddess. And not in a harem pants, namaste, yoga class kind of way. (No shade to that lifestyle, but it's just not what we're talking about here!)

I mean this as in, **you are literally a goddess with the power to create and destroy at the ends of your beautifully manicured fingertips.** You choose what you see through those glossy black eyelashes. You attract lovers, girl gangs, and abundance with your vibration. Your thoughts become things, your words are wands, and your energy is everything.

That's the good news. You are INFINITELY more powerful than you think!

And the bad news? You are INFINITELY more powerful than you think! So any suffering you commit to, any unpleasantries to which you are handcuffed, any pity parties you throw... These are entirely your creation. The more you engage with them, the deeper you crawl into them, the heavier they become. The more real and tangible they are.

Robert Anton Wilson once said, "The mind is a tool invented by the Universe to see itself." In short, we are constant magicians. We possess the power of the infinite Universe within us. We are creating the conditions of our lives.

No matter what is going on in your life, it is important that you claim it, take ownership of it, and understand that it is something you conjured into being.

Believe me when I say that the Universe has not pinned a "Kick me" sign to your back. You are not cursed, destined for misery, or a victim of cosmic malpractice. Your so-called "bad luck" is a creation of your own! (Gasp!)

Once you start to grasp this fact, really bite into it, gnash it with your teeth, lick and taste and begin to digest it, reality as you know it looks radically different.

You will have begun to realize that *your reality* is your creation.

This can be a bittersweet pill to swallow. Who doesn't want to take credit for all the positive things in their life?! All those scrumptious orgasms, killer outfits, beautiful panoramas... Yes! A hearty, full-body yes to these things!

But we're less keen to acknowledge that those depressing relationships, dead-end jobs, and nasty frenemies could be our responsibility too.

We can't have it both ways. Either we're responsible for *everything*—even the things we don't understand, that have caused us pain—or we're not responsible for anything at all. And application of a lil' thing called logic simply does not co-sign the idea that our lives are the result of random chance.

Look at the people in your life and the things they tell themselves on a daily basis. What stories do they insist on telling, what beliefs do they hold, what do they think about all the time? If the conditions of their lives are not an absolute match to these things, I will donate all my clothes to charity and go naked for the rest of my life!

These things do not happen by chance. We are not "fated" to anything!

If you are reading this, I know that you want more for yourself. You want to unfurl your petals like a lotus flower. I am here to help you see that you can do this, that it is easy!

But you have to start by letting go of your old beliefs. You have to stop telling yourself disempowering stories that keep you locked into your dissatisfying past, stories that rationalize the dissatisfying conditions of your present, stories that will justify the dissatisfying outcomes of your future. You have to stop spending time with people who reinforce these patterns, who enable you, or who try to dim your light at every opportunity possible. And you have to take responsibility for purposefully crafting your own life.

This is a bold new world. A world where everything is possible. Where your dreams are never too big. Where you feel delicious in your body, your smile lights up the room, and you feel inspired, grateful, and excited every single day.

This is not a far-fetched fantasy. It can be your reality right now!

All you have to do is decide. Decide that this is who you are now. Decide that this is what you believe.

You actually do not have to "earn" a life that feels good. You do not have to continue flagellating yourself by constantly digging for fresh pain or desperately trying to heal something that was never broken in the first place. You don't have to insist on your unworthiness, or that you're fractured and lost.

What if I told you that you are absolutely perfect right now?

Could you accept it? Could you take it in? Or would it just piss you off?

There is a lot of money to be made in assuring people that they are damaged and that they need help. Whether it's a juice cleanse, a spiritual retreat or a new sports car, businesses thrive when they insist that you are not enough and that this thing, finally, this one thing, will fix you! It will assuredly make you feel whole and complete and good about yourself! And for only 25 easy payments of $499.99!

You know what? No. Let's start to tell ourselves that we are beautiful, talented geniuses. Let's affirm that we are wonderful right now, no interference required. Let's accept that we are constantly creating with our thoughts and our feelings, so it's important that we choose them intentionally and we set ourselves up for success!

LEARNING HOW TO THINK

Envision the things you want—your desires—as beautifully-wrapped gifts, and your feelings as a conveyor belt. Every time you think of something you want, your mind spits it out as a pretty present and it drops onto the conveyor belt of how you feel. Now, what is the role of the conveyor belt?

Your feelings dictate the speed with which your manifestation will come to fruition. Your feelings can speed the conveyor belt up, they can slow it down, and they can even turn you in the other direction if someone hits the switch. So how you are feeling lets you know whether you are getting closer to, or further away from, what you want. As you can probably imagine, feeling good speeds you closer. Feeling negative, doubtful, or impatient slows down the whole process. If you stay in an unpleasant frame of mind for months, years, or decades, it could even knock the gift off the belt entirely!

This is because the ultimate goal is to get into vibrational alignment with what you want. *Delicious things require delicious feelings.* It's really as simple as that.

Your feelings are your lighthouse. They are your guide. People get really tripped up on whether their manifestations are "working," and the only way to know is to appraise your feelings. If you feel mostly good, what you want is on its way! But if you feel mostly bad, you are veering off course.

When I started to consistently practice this idea, I was absolutely shocked by how often I was feeling pessimistic, disappointed, angry, or hopeless. I had been thinking of myself as a positive person for the last decade, but it was staggering to realize that I was in a deeply negative state multiple times a day! (Of course, then I wondered why certain parts of my life just kept getting worse and worse! As you now know, whatever we put our attention on grows!)

As you begin to work with these concepts, you, like me, may also be surprised by how regularly you feel bad. That's okay. Simply notice it and breathe. Feeling guilty or ashamed, or beating yourself up for having a negative feeling is not going to get you to where you want to go any faster, so let go of the guilt or shame as soon as you can. Allow yourself to feel your emotions without judgment, let it move through you, and then watch with fascination as it drops to the floor! Science has shown us that we can only physically feel an emotion for 90 seconds— so you might be amazed by how quickly the feeling dissipates!

Release yourself from the burden of feeling guilty or ashamed about *any* of this. You are not expected to know! Very few, if any of us, are taught about these ideas as children. It's so unfortunate, because imagine how empowered we would have been if we'd known these things from a young age! Imagine what the world would look like if people truly understood that their feelings are guiding *everything* in their lives? Most adults are completely unaware of how much control they have. We have no idea how to think or harness our true creative power. If we're lucky, we might be taught critical thinking in school, but what about thinking for self-love? Thinking for manifestation?

Most of us have a habit of following our feelings wherever they deign to take us. Since our mind is primal in nature, and the fear part of our brain is so overly-developed in order to survive, we all have a tendency to veer towards the negative. To fixate on problems. To imagine the worst-case scenario, and stay there.

Back in the days of furry loincloths and chewing wooly mammoth meat off the bone, this was perfectly fine. It served a beautiful purpose. We needed that acute sense of fear to keep us alive and to propagate the species. But these days... Not so much. Most of us are living in the lap of luxury, chilling with our wifi and climate control, chugging back lattes and ordering sequin catsuits online. (Wait, is that just me?!) The truth about today is that life is just not that dangerous. The biggest threat to our lives is walking out in front of a car while glued to our phone!

The problem is that the limbic system—the "Watch out! Halt there! DANGER AHEAD!" part of our brain— is still super-active. And, how do I put this? It's a little bored! It's twiddling its thumbs, desperate for a saber-toothed tiger or tsunami. So it gets its kicks by creating mayhem and mischief in our essentially peaceful lives.

Instead of fearing prehistoric predators, now we're afraid of public speaking. Being authentic. Getting rejected. Being criticized. And our minds are in total overdrive.

These intense fears are hard-wired into our biology, so we are probably not going to be able to completely wipe them out within the next 100 years. But we can give ourselves a chance at serenity and happiness by simply realizing this is how we are programmed. We get to choose whether we listen to these messages and we get to input new messages, more empowering messages, into our minds at will.

IT'S A GOOD DAY TO HAVE A GOOD DAY

Let's start with the morning. It's a fresh beginning, a new dawn. How glorious!

Many of us dream about having a beautiful start to our day. We'd wake up with the sunrise, hear the birds chirping, stretch, meditate, and float into the shower. Or perhaps you fantasize about sleeping in, your lover bringing you a triple-shot espresso, and having a delicious romp in the sheets before tackling the day ahead. We all have a different idea of what the ideal morning could look like, but one thing is for certain: none of us dream about waking up feeling groggy, being late, and tripping over a pile of shoes left inconveniently in front of the door!

Why is this? Well, no one wants to feel bad. And we also know, deep down, that how the morning begins is likely to affect the rest of our day. That old saying about "waking up on the wrong side of the bed" is really a self-fulfilling prophecy for some people!

Here's how the morning plays out from an energetic standpoint. You are essentially starting at zero. While you slept, all the momentum—by which I mean all the energy you generated during the day before—came to a halt. You were dreaming, regenerating, rebuilding your cells, fixing and repairing. Your subconscious mind was essentially giving you therapy, figuring out the nitty-gritty of your problems. (This is one of the reasons why people tell you to "sleep on" a problem: your subconscious is working to provide solutions in the mind overnight!) So when you wake up, you are at zilch. Your energy is purely neutral. As you open your eyes, you are being presented with a beautiful blank canvas upon which you can project *anything you like.*

The vibe of your day will follow the vibe of your morning. So with this in mind, it makes sense to set up your home and your life so that you are giving yourself the best possible start!

Once your eyes flutter open, the first thing you do is take in the sights around you. Sitting here, reading this, right now, take a moment to ask yourself: What is on my bedside table? What art is on the walls in my bedroom? How could I cultivate a happier scene and create more pleasure? You see, even the smallest tweaks to our seemingly routine lives can impact us enormously.

Personally, I am a paradox. I love things and I am such a magpie, and yet at the same time, I always feel better when I am not faced with clutter. It seems like I spent my twenties snapping up everything that took my fancy, which led to delightfully overflowing bookshelves and a truly unruly closet. While this was certainly fun to look at (maximalism forever!), it was also a little bit... stressful.

Now, in my thirties, I am experimenting with buying fewer things and being far more discerning. When I moved into my new home I ONLY bought things I loved to fill it. If I couldn't find the right item, I would not buy it. This is such a simple idea but makes such a huge difference!

Here are a few things I like to do which add to the joy of my morning, and that you might like to incorporate too.

♥ At night, before I go to sleep, I silence my phone, light candles, and allow myself to wind down. This helps me sleep more soundly, which adds to my feelings of positivity and well-restedness in the morning. ♥ I like to read before I fall asleep, and I do this as often as possible. ♥ Being warm really helps me relax, so I love to submerge myself in the tub with some Epsom salts, or lie on my infrared mat filled with pieces of amethyst. Blissful! ♥ I tidy up my home every night before I go to sleep. That way, there's nothing distracting or messy to my eye, and there is no better feeling than waking up to a clean house. ♥ I don't often use an alarm, but when I do, I either set it to cheerful birdsong or make sure it's a song that I love! ♥ Stack items that remind you of who you want to be on your bedside table: a journal, a canteen of fresh water, crystals to meditate with. ♥ I set crystal rainbow makers in my windows, so that when the sun hits them, rainbows dance around my room. (Light clears the energy in a space, so every time these rainbows circulate, I see it as an energetic sweep.) ♥

Now, let's talk about your mindset. This is where it starts to get juicy!

THE MOMENTUM OF YOUR MORNING MIND

We are constantly building momentum. We are either pouring fuel on the fire of something good, or we're stoking the flames of the things we are most afraid of. It all depends on where you're putting your attention.

We are not actually at the mercy of our thoughts, like we think we are. That's just a trick our brain is playing on us! We get to choose our thoughts, and we also get to choose how long we spend with each one. I see our brains as an endless series of trampolines, stretching as far as the eye can see. Each trampoline represents a thought: "I'm ugly" or "Life is beautiful" or "I'll never be loved." The wonderful thing about our minds is that we get to choose which trampoline we bounce to, and how long we jump up and down on it. The longer we jump, the deeper we go. Want to feel good? Bounce on a joyful thought! Want to feel like a piece of gum stuck to an old shoe? Bounce on a thought of scarcity, fear, or lack!

As Abraham-Hicks says, "We are so free that we can choose bondage." So if you want to choose a thought that makes you feel bad, that builds those negative emotions, that encourages fear within you, you absolutely have the right to do so! However... May I suggest that you'd probably be happier if you chose a more fulfilling thought?!

It's essential that we choose the right thoughts first thing in the morning. When you wake up, it's as if the opening credits of a movie are just starting to roll. You get to decide: is this a tense drama? A romantic comedy? A musical? A surreal art-house flick?

Imagine your morning as if it is an old-fashioned set of scales, with a little cup dangling from each end. On one side, you have good feelings (which lead to positive manifestations.) On the other, you have negative feelings (which lead to... You guessed it!) When you wake up, both sides of the scale are empty, but the gift of the day is that your pockets are full of thousands of tiny little pebbles— thoughts—to fill them up with. If you start to load up the negative side, it gets heavier and heavier. You begin to stay there. To dwell. To go down the rabbit-hole. But it's just as easy to start stacking your pebbles on the positive side!

Your first thoughts in the morning lean you in one direction or the other, and from there, momentum builds. Your positive or negative thoughts gain impetus, and start to drive you forward. You have probably experienced this yourself many times: when you wake up and instantly think something negative, your day simply goes downhill from there. On the other hand, when you wake up feeling grateful, it gets better!

Now, before you start telling yourself some kind of silly story, for example, 'I'm just a negative person', stop right there! No, you're not. That's a limiting belief, and quite frankly, an excuse for lazy thinking. Let's demand more from ourselves! We *all* have the ability to go negative, just like we all have the ability to go positive! We each have just as many negative thoughts as we do positive ones. You only think more negative thoughts because this is a pattern you have trained yourself into. It is a routine. Don't get it twisted: you are capable of thinking thousands of positive thoughts a day, you are just not as well-practiced!

This is why having some kind of morning practice—an opportunity to set yourself up for positivity—is so essential. It almost doesn't matter what the practice is, as long as you have one!

I heard a recording from a seminar a couple of months ago, where someone in the audience said, "When I wake up, I like to think of my day as a song. Do I want it to be energetic and loud? Or soft and gentle? And then I think thoughts and take actions that will get me there." I loved this idea.

The good news is that even if you wake up with an unpleasant thought, it is still early in the day! You can choose to switch your thinking. When we do this, when we behave preemptively and take initiative, we are actually taking action so that we are not at the mercy of our *reactions*. Great, huh?

This is one of the reasons why people suggest that you meditate in the morning. Your mind is more open, more malleable, and if you take a moment to sit in stillness, it will set a gentle tone for the rest of your day.

My morning routine is as follows.

Most days, I let the sun coming through my skylight wake me up. (This is such a privilege after living in NYC for a decade. I am grateful every time it happens, even if I sometimes wish I could get a little more sleep!) I snuggle with my dogs, make myself an oat milk latte, put on some music, and sit down with my purple journal to do my morning pages. I write at least three pages by hand, and it's incredible how much clarity I get from this simple process! Sometimes I do this at the kitchen counter, and sometimes I sit on my balcony where I can breathe the ocean air and enjoy the sun on my back. Once my coffee has kicked in, I change into workout clothes, head downstairs, and get a great sweat going on my Peloton bike! Starting my day like this is so powerful, and is my favorite version of my morning routine so far.

The next step is my Magical Morning Practice, which you'll learn about below.

MAGICAL MORNING: THE PRACTICE

If your desires are gifts and your feelings move the gift either closer or further away, where does your behavior come into play?

Your behavior, or the things you do and the words you say, are an extension of your *feelings*. If you feel happy, you will do happy things! It is really that simple. No one expects words of comfort from an angry person, just like you'll never see a truly blissful person biting the head off a pigeon! So it is essential that we get ourselves into a positive place every morning.

The way you act—whether you are kind to your postman and smile at your barista, or walk around with a bad attitude—absolutely reverberates throughout your life! You would be off your tree to think that there are no consequences to acting like a dick. Trust me, there are!

If you're ever in doubt, simply remember this:

We do not attract what we would like, we attract what we are like.

This concept shows up when we are interacting with the world—ever feel like everyone is rude when you're in a bad mood?—and it also means that it is important that we get into *vibrational alignment* with the things that we want in our lives. If you want a big house but you're swollen with unworthiness, you will never get it. If you want to fall in love but you're convinced of your unlovability, guess what? It ain't coming!

Years ago, I created something called the Magical Morning Practice. At the time, I was going through a really rough patch with my aforementioned boyfriend, and I needed something to help me focus on what was good and possible. This practice was the result, and it's an absolute super-highway to manifesting all the things you desire!

The Magical Morning Practice gets us onto the same *emotional track* as the things that we want. In our Magical Mornings, we speak about things as if they have already happened, so that our subconscious mind can accept them as done, and set about pulling levers and making them happen. When we speak in the past tense, we give our bodies and minds an opportunity to accept these things as done and complete.

It's the difference between walking past Gucci and staring in the window excitedly... And sashaying into the store, trying on a pair of sunglasses, and taking a cute selfie in them! Putting ourselves into the picture helps us feel that whatever we want is easy to obtain, and that whatever we want is already ours. It is much easier to act "as if" when we get intimate and close with whatever we want to manifest. This massively speeds up our vibrational alignment!

The Magical Morning Practice is so easy that it almost feels criminal, especially when you realize how quickly it works! But the more I learn about manifesting, the more I realize that it is all about ease! Letting it flow is essential, and the root of everything good.

For this practice, I like to use my phone as a magical tool. Besides, we are pretty much all addicted to our phones, and even though we know we shouldn't be using them as soon as we roll over and open our eyes, hands up if you still do this every single morning. (Yeah... Me too!) So instead of lambasting ourselves for this grave offense, why not use the phone as a tool to do something positive?

STEP 1: Pick up your phone and open whatever app you have to record a voice memo. Hit record, and start talking.

STEP 2: Speak about what you're grateful for. Dive deep into this! Get high on the countless blessings that are already in your life, from the frozen coffee drink in your hand to the art show you saw last week. Let your feelings guide you as you do this—it is not supposed to be an intellectual or logical exercise. The only way to get the full benefit from this is if you really FEEL into it, luxuriate in each item you mention, and allow yourself to expound on everything with glee. Every time you do this, it will feel different. Some days, you will express your gratitude with violent enthusiasm and excitement. On other days, the gratitude will feel more like relief and calmness. And there will be days where it falls somewhere in between those two ends of the spectrum. All of this is wonderful and okay. Allow yourself to ride the waves of emotionality. They are a gift of being human. Talk about what you're grateful for until you feel that it has raised your frequency; that you're not just thinking about what's good, you actually feel it.

STEP 3: Now, talk about your desire for the day. I love this step because until I started doing this on a daily basis, I felt very disconnected from my desires. Before Magical Morning, my "desire" was to tick items off my to-do list... And there's very little pleasure in that. My life motto now is PLEASURE OVER EVERYTHING, and in order to live this as opposed to just thinking it, it's essential that I get in touch with what I really, truly want. This process is going to open your eyes to what you actually desire, which is so much fun!

Here's the kicker: you are going to phrase all of this in the PAST TENSE.

You will say, "I wrote 3000 words and it was amazing!" Instead of, "I'm going to write 3000 words today!"

You are going to talk about it as if it is already a done deal: signed, sealed, and delivered. As if it was an old story you were telling your grandchildren... Channel that old lady on the Titanic! Or tell it as if you're on a top 10 podcast and you have the host eating out of the palm of your hand!

You are going to look back at your day—yes, your day which has not happened yet!—and tell the story of it.

Mine might sound like this.

"I had such a beautiful day. The weather was perfect, and after I did my morning routine, I went for a walk along the beach. I felt so good in my outfit and strong in my body! I had this lovely conversation with my man that made us feel closer than ever, and we planned some adventures for the future that we are both so excited about. Then I drove in to Los Angeles to be on a podcast, and it went so well—maybe the best interview I've ever done! By the time I got home again, I was feeling so full of life. I laughed with my friend as I drove home, and fell asleep dreaming about my man."

You can be really specific with this if that feels good. But you can also be more vague if that feels good! A less-specific desire might sound like this...

"I had such a beautiful day. I woke up feeling great, and then something happened that surprised and delighted me even more! I attracted a magnificent opportunity that I had been hoping for for a long time. And I went to bed feeling peaceful and magnificent."

STEP 4: Finally, talk about your future desires. Again, you are going to phrase this in the past tense. This is the place where you get to go really BIG. Take a moment to zoom out on your life—Google Earth style—and see what is possible. (Hint: ANYTHING is possible!) Remember to say it as if it has already happened.

Say, "I'm so happy I bought the house of my dreams!"

Not, "I'm so happy I am buying the house of my dreams!"

Or, "I'm so happy that I am about to buy the house of my dreams!"

So, an example of this segment might go something like this.

"For my future desire... I'm so happy that I bought my dream house in California with a view of the ocean and an infinity pool. I love flying off to Hawaii every month to be with my man and enjoy being in nature together. I love driving the car of my dreams around with my friends, and going on road trips with people I love. I'm so happy to be in love with the most incredible man and that our relationship is so easy and joyful. My business keeps expanding in the most beautiful and surprising ways, I'm creative every day, the money flows constantly, and I keep doing bigger and more fun things all the time."

Yum. It felt good just writing that! Speaking it out loud is even more powerful, and sharing it with someone else brings it rushing into the present moment with even more vigor. Which brings me to...

STEP 5: You're done! Stop recording. Now it's time to save the voice note, and send it to a friend! YES! Does that sound scary? I know that it might, but it's a really big piece of this process. This person is going to become your manifestation buddy. They are going to hold your hand throughout this process, and be by your side.

There are a few reasons for sharing. One is that it encourages you to be bold and unashamed about what you want. So many of us have guilt over the things that we want and this is like extreme aversion therapy: it pushes us to get over that!

The second reason is that when you share your dreams with other people, you'll begin to realize that *they are not really a big deal.* The things you want aren't that crazy or out of reach at all!

And finally, involving someone else in your Magical Morning is beautiful because it amplifies the strength of the transmission. When I listen to my friends' recordings, which can range from 5-10 minutes long, I am often doing something else: putting on make-up, tidying up, etc. As I listen, I am paying attention, but not absolute attention... And this means that I am visualizing *everything* they say as being done already. I'm not always sure what section we're in: gratitude or desire? This makes it even more real! In my mind's eye, I can see my friend doing that thing she wants to do! In my imagination, it is already manifested. This helps me give her really enthusiastic feedback and it boosts the signal of her manifestations.

You should note that the Magical Morning Practice is not just a cute name— this is truly a magical practice! Be mindful about who you invite in. You might wish you could bring your best friend into it, but secretly, deep down, you know that they won't be fully supportive and they certainly won't be able to be vulnerable enough to respond in kind. If this is how you feel, don't send the message to them. What I recommend is floating the idea with a few friends who you think would be into it, and then test it out. See how it feels. (This is always the ultimate test: how does it feel?)

STEP 6: Anticipate your friend's delicious message in return. As I progress with this practice, I've discovered that the most joyful Magical Morning exchanges occur when you both give a little bit of feedback on what the other has sent through.

Now, by feedback, I do not mean unsolicited opinions. What I mean is that you upride your friend's message, and they do the same to you. An upride is when you hear someone and you encourage them, you support them, you uplift them. This could be as simple as, "I'm so happy you did so much writing, it sounded so satisfying! I loved it!" Or you can get more advanced with it, and ENHANCE their vision. So you might say, "I love your new car too, and it was so fun driving with you up the Pacific Coast Highway!" Have fun with it.

OTHER NOTES

This is a deeply transformative practice and if you commit to it consistently, you will truly be astounded by the changes that occur. It is the fastest manifestation tool I have ever used, by a country mile.

You can, of course, do this practice any time of day, but I love it in the morning because it really kicks you off on the right foot. Sometimes I do it in bed, sometimes I pace around my house, but when I lived in New York City, I would do it while I walked my dog in the East Village!

If you don't feel comfortable sharing your manifestations with someone else, you don't have to at first. Just make the recordings and save them for yourself. You could even make a practice of listening to them at the end of the day to "check in" and see whether your manifestations are hitting the mark! But I recommend that eventually, you make the leap and you find a buddy to exchange Magical Mornings with.

If this exercise makes you feel uncomfortable, that's even more of a reason to do it. We often resist the ideas that we know, deep-down, will encourage us to grow, get bigger, and be bolder. And as much as I am an enthusiastic proponent of this technique, you will not see results from just reading or hearing about it! Only life experience teaches. In other words, you'll never know if you never give it a go!

So go on! No matter what time of day it is, crack open your voice memo app and make your first recording!

IN CONCLUSION

"The body becomes what the foods are; as the spirit becomes what the thoughts are."—Ancient Kemetic Proverb

I am so proud of you for embarking on this journey. Make no mistake: as we work through this book together, you will overhaul your entire life. It is going to be *incredible*. And you are not doing it alone!

There is an entire community of badass babes reading this book and making huge changes to their lives, and I've created a library of support for you to call on whenever you desire it! Go to galadarling.com and click on the **Book Bonuses** tab to get access to the whole lot. You'll find guided tapping videos and so much more—absolutely free!

As you watch the videos, you're welcome to and share what's going on for you. We are in this together... And we're a very big, very powerful group! Lean on us!

In this chapter, we have examined a lot of ideas that may be at odds with some of your long-held views about life, and that may have felt challenging. That's okay. You may find, as I said, that you are shocked by how much negativity you are feeling. That's okay too! It is only by becoming aware that we can truly begin to make changes. This is phase one, and there is so much to come.

Start to pay attention to your feelings. Do whatever it takes to make yourself feel good in the morning, commit to the Magical Morning Practice for 31 days, and see how your life begins to shift.

Things are only going to get better. Just you wait. ✳

"Wanting to feel good is synonymous with wanting to feel God." —Wayne Dyer

02

FEELING GOOD
IS YOUR JOB

W E ARE A GENERATION OF SEEKERS. WE SPEND OUR time looking for more, wanting answers. We saw the way our parents lived their lives, mostly on a constant quest of providing for their families, and we know that *there is more.*

Some of us go looking for it in drugs, sex, ego, and acquisition. When we realize that those things don't work, that they provide no true balm for our soul, no soothing of our existential angst, we look elsewhere. Yoga. Family. Spirituality. Meditation. Travel. Loving. Serving. Creating.

We think a lot about our purpose in life. Why are we here? What's our mission? How can we serve the world? These are beautiful questions which come from a good place, but in a lot of ways, they are misguided. They are a roundabout way to reach an inherently simple truth.

Your job, your purpose, your mission, and the reason you are here is to feel joy.

You are here to taste the rainbow of life, with all its contrasting experiences. To feel a kaleidoscope of multitudes. To bear witness to awe-inspiring things that open your mind. And to allow these moments to help you create new desires.

The goal is to continually experience more joy. To desire things and then bring them to glorious fruition. To experience connection with yourself. To be in the present, and enjoy it so much that it brings even more ecstasy rushing into your life.

The only rule when it comes to your vocation is that it should help feed your delight. It should allow you to build upon your happiness, to experience more satisfaction. *Feeling good must always be your first priority.* You are no use to the world when you are operating from a place of sadness or scarcity.

So let's investigate this idea of feeling good, especially as it relates to manifestation.

One of the common misconceptions about manifesting is that we have to really OBSESS and white-knuckle grip our vision of how it could be. You may be relieved to hear that this is precisely the opposite of what works!

Here's how it actually goes down.

You think of something you want, and as soon as the desire is born within you, the Universe conjures it up. Just like a solution is always created in tandem with a problem, *so your desire is always created in tandem with its tangible result.*

Trust this: as soon as you ask, it is given. It materializes, thanks to the Universe. You do not have to worry about that. IT EXISTS. Bam!

You may be thinking, 'Well, that sounds great. But how come the thing I want—the hot love, the bulging bank balance, the bangin' bod—isn't in my living room?'

It's not in your living room because this is a question of *vibrational alignment.* By this I mean, you have to feel how this thing feels, on a consistent basis, in order for it to show up in tangible form. So your job is simply to relax, act as if you already have it, and allow it to come to you.

My dear friend (and therapist) Terri Cole explains manifesting like this: As soon as she has an idea of what she wants, the Universe places it on a (metaphorical) UPS truck, on its way to her.

Think about that for a second. We often agonize over whether something is coming or not, whether it is happening or not, when it will show up, etc. This can be a real trip. We keep checking our watch, thinking about our biological clock, watching other people get what they want and feeling internally petulant that our time has not yet come.

Have you ever heard the saying, "A watched pot never boils?" (I think this is actually an old wives' version of the double slit experiment in quantum physics, but no matter!) Have you noticed that this notion is true?! Let's upgrade this saying to something we can all really understand. A watched phone never dings! A constantly-refreshed inbox never delivers a job offer. A pressured lover never produces an engagement ring!

Let's come back to this UPS truck analogy. Think about the last time you ordered something online. Allow me to take you on a trip, using a sequin catsuit as our example! In this story, you were perusing the site, with lots of things jockeying for your attention, but you were most drawn to the sequin catsuit. (I mean, who wouldn't be?!) Your eyes were completely agog! Your jaw was on the floor! So you placed your order. The website sent you a shipping notification and a tracking link, how kind. But you already know that those tracking links never work! Somehow, the journey between "Dispatched from warehouse" and "Signed delivery" is like staring into the abyss. As much as the tracking is supposed to update you, it *rarely* does. You might refresh that page five times a day, but it still won't give you any more information! AND YET... You still trust and believe that the sequin catsuit is on its way to you. You're already thinking about how you will feel once you shimmy into it and sashay around the house.

You're already fantasizing about how to photograph it and show its maximum potential. You are absolutely in alignment with this catsuit, and more to the point, you have absolute faith that it will show up at your house. You asked, and it was given. So all that you can do is be happy about it, clear space in your closet, and fantasize about what shoes and wig will match it best.

This is the best way I can explain manifesting to you! As soon as you decide that you want it, you launch a "rocket of desire" (as Abraham-Hicks says). In this precise moment, that thing springs into being. Then, your only work is to enjoy life, relax, and feel good as often as possible so that the thing you want can float into your experience.

Have you ever noticed that the things you want only come when you are *happy*?! It's true, isn't it? When you're moping around hoping your crush will text you, your phone stays silent! But when you're out and about, enjoying life, having the best time possible, that's when they slide into your DMs, all cute and hopeful!

When you feel good, you radiate those feelings outwards. You are literally a magnet, pulling in people, things, and experiences. And when you feel desperate and lonely, you reap more of the same. You refresh your phone to no avail. All quiet on the Western front!

By the way, it is completely normal to have these ups and downs. After I moved to LA, I was feeling good, but the changes were so big that it threw my momentum off. I was rushing, feeling very "busy" and a little bit overwhelmed—even while being grateful for all the good things in my life. So I felt good, but it wasn't very *consistent*. Emotionally, I was lurching from feeling good to feeling burdened, from being grateful to being stressed out.

The key to manifesting is to maintain a sense of *stability* in our frequency as much as possible. I noticed that my vibration was a bit all over the place and I took steps to get back into that high vibe feeling. I restarted my Magical Morning Practice. I recommitted to going to the gym and walking between two and four miles every day. I turned my mornings into a delicious ritual that amplified my frequency. And what happened?

About two days later, three—yes three—of my exes got back in touch. I was so happy to hear from all of them! They are all lovely people. I saw one of them the next day, and I made plans with the other to see them at the end of the month!

Coincidence? Actually, yes, but only because the true definition of coincidence is the precise opposite of how we use it today! The word coincidence is from the Medieval Latin *coincidere*, which literally means "to fall upon together!"

There is no separation of the areas of your life. They are intrinsically intertwined. Everything that you do in your life feeds everything else. You are not operating as a solo voyager. Everything is connected. When you take care of your frequency, people are drawn in. When you spend time with people you like, things happen quickly! When you take inspired action, your life just works.

On the flip-side, if you neglect your health, and if you refuse to tend to your own vibration, you will feel stuck and stagnant. You will never get to experience the things you dream about. There is too far a way to go, vibrationally. It is like trying to push a boulder up a hill. It's too much work.

What you want to do instead is get the ball rolling by feeling good in the morning, and allow those positive feelings to build, so that you are in energetic alignment with the things you want. They will come to you *so much more quickly*.

I started working with a new client in the Philippines recently. As we talked, she revealed to me that she was worried that we would create endless "action plans" that made her feel stressed out and anxious. Imagine her relief when I told her that her only homework is to FEEL GOOD and BE RADIANT!

It's your homework too!

One of the most challenging parts of manifesting is maintaining a consistent vibration. We hop back and forth between, "I'm so excited about this!" and, "What if I never get it?" We jump from, "It will be so good!" to "Why isn't it here yet?" This is like constantly fiddling with the dial on your radio—not that anyone has those anymore. But fiddling with the dial means you get some Top 40 and then some static, a blaring infomercial and then a little more static. The goal is to keep your dial—or frequency—as steady as possible, like a perfectly-tuned radio.

WHAT DOES IT MEAN TO FEEL GOOD?

Many of us are living in an unconscious way. We are not even really aware of our feelings, having been encouraged by today's society to essentially ignore them in favor of "getting things done." But our feelings and emotions are actually essential! When we pay attention to them, they don't just help us figure out what we want from life, they also work as a guide, showing us how close we are to those things we want to manifest.

When you decide that you want to feel good as often as you can, you will start to have more awareness of how you feel. I must warn you: at the beginning of this journey, you will probably find yourself feeling terrible more often than not! This might surprise you. It shocked the hell out of me! As I started to pay attention to my moods, it was wild to realize how often I was feeling cranky, irritated, bored, demotivated, apathetic, or angry. I was stunned to realize that I felt that way *all the time!*

Learning to get a handle on your emotions can be a rollercoaster, but it is such an important thing to do. A lot of us have learned to shut down our emotions, often because of what transpired in our family home. As a result, we feel we don't have a "right" to experience our own emotions, and so we start to live from the neck up: cerebral, logical, and kind of emotionally flat.

If you've decided that it might be time to bust out the ol' feelings, you might be scared of doing so. Personally, I had a lot of resistance to doing this, because I was afraid of what might come up. But do you know what I discovered that is so fascinating?

When we allow ourselves to feel an emotion *fully*—by which I mean we throw our arms wide open and say, 'Okay, let me experience the totality of this, no holds barred!'—science has proven that we can only *physically* feel that emotion for 90 seconds maximum!

Isn't that incredible? I avoided my feelings for the better part of 20 years, all to realize that those emotions would only have activated me for 90 seconds at most!

Your feelings are simply information, and they are not the boss of you. You might have a fear that you are at the mercy of your feelings: like they are just something that is happening to you.

But nothing could be further from the truth.

You are totally in control of your moods, your feelings, and your emotions. The more that you pay attention to them, the more you will realize this is true. You will start to be able to step outside of them and play detective. 'Hmmm, I'm feeling pissed off. When did this begin? Well, I was really irritated by how this person spoke to me, and then I let that affect me, and the reason that *really* bothers me is because of this thing from my childhood...' You will start to become aware of what triggers you, and most crucially, you will realize that the way you respond to those triggers is a choice too!

It's said that our first thought is involuntary. It is something that is deeply programmed and in essence, inescapable (although I believe this is something you can rewire through tapping, hypnosis, etc.). But your second thought? Your second thought is something you can train.

Some people believe that the mind is a cage. I don't subscribe to this. The mind is only a cage if you do not know how to use it effectively. If you have learned how to use it, and you practice doing so, then your mind is the key to the kingdom!

You are fully in charge of how you feel and what you think. This is the genesis of everything else. Your life is an extension of your mind. You only need to look around at the conditions of your life to see that this is absolutely true. Seeing is believing, as they say. If your life is awash with miserable people, a crappy job, no money in the bank, a passionless relationship and poor health, you can bet your bottom dollar that your mind had an enormous part in the making of it.

I would go so far as to say that your mind is, in fact, 100% responsible for creating this life as it stands today.

If you're looking around at your life feeling deeply dissatisfied, don't blame yourself or beat yourself up. After all, as my hero Louise Hay once said, "You have been criticizing yourself for years, and it hasn't worked! Try approving of yourself instead." We cannot punish our way into a more beautiful life—this much I know for sure.

Be gentle with yourself. Self-love is always the solution to your problems. And remember: transformation begins with willingness, this is not permanent, and if you change your thoughts, you can change your world.

Learning to think differently, to discipline our minds, to use them in a way that is constructive and not destructive, is emotional fitness. It is something that NO ONE teaches us! And it is the most important thing we can ever learn: to harness the immense power of our minds so that we can live beautiful lives. But since no one teaches it, it is up to us to learn it, practice it, and teach others.

Emotional fitness is about mental discipline. We really have no idea what we should be doing with our brains. We let our fears run amok and create the movies in our heads, which then prevent us from doing what we really want. Undisciplined thinking is our utmost downfall. We have an unpleasant thought and we just keep following it! Often we don't even consider stepping away from it: it floats into our consciousness, so we follow it down the rabbit-hole. And we all know what happens when we keep following those unhappy thoughts: nothing good!

It takes practice, discipline, and radical self-awareness to notice when you are doing this with your mind. The good news is that now you have read these words, you are no longer asleep. You are aware of what is happening in your mind. And now you have the power to flip the damn script!

As I was saying, when you begin this process, you will notice that your unpleasant feelings linger for a long time. As The Cranberries once sang, "Do you have to, do you have to, do you have to let it linger?" And the answer, of course, is no. You do not, in fact, have to let it linger!

Soon you will have such awareness of your moods that you will grow totally intolerant of anything but feeling good. You will realize that if you don't feel good, there is only one thing to do: get back to feeling good!

'Okay smartypants,' I hear you thinking. (Yes, I am that psychic.) 'If I don't feel good, what am I supposed to do so that I can start feeling good?'

The answer is this: you have to use your body. We are seldom able to think ourselves into a better mood. You have to disrupt your patterns by using physical movement!

Some of my favorite ways to bust out of a bad mood include tapping, chasing my dogs around, going for a drive, meditation, napping, having an orgasm (or three), working out, going for a walk, dancing in my living room, singing, journaling, or writing a gratitude list. All of these activities shake up my energetic body, which in turn changes my physical body, which then affects my emotional state. Emotion is created by motion, and your physiology determines your psychology. In short, if you don't feel good, move your body!

Occasionally women will write to me and say that they cannot possibly feel good in a bad moment because they have children. No! This is an excuse at best. In fact, your children give you an even better reason to model beautiful behavior so that they can grow up and know how to manage their own emotions! If you're cranky—or they are!—why not give them the incredible gift of teaching them how easy and fast it is to change their mood? They will immediately soak up these lessons, and if you continue to reinforce them, these will become part of their essential life skills!

If you're having a tough time, involve your children in this process of feeling good. Dance together, sing together, do jumping jacks together. Ask them how they feel afterwards! Let them connect the dots. This is one of the best gifts you can give them.

Another common question I get asked is, "When I'm cranky, sometimes I don't even WANT to feel good. I just want to indulge in my bad mood. Why does this happen, and what can I do about it?"

This is simply a bad old habit, and feeling miserable is familiar to you. You have to break this pattern if you want to create a new life for yourself, and the only way to change your mood is to take action! No one else can do it for you, so this is on you. It is up to you to change your mood, so no matter how irritated you're feeling, it is up to YOU to play Beyonce at ear-melting volume, it is up to YOU to twerk on the floor until you start laughing, it is up to YOU to tap until you feel calm again!

It is really that simple: just take action and stop making excuses!

If you're on the fence about whether you want to wallow or let it go, remember that everything we feel attracts similar experiences. Every emotion that passes through us draws in people, moments and situations that vibrate at a similar frequency. The longer we allow a feeling to percolate, the stronger its pull. Think of it like powering up a magnet. Do you want to charge it with positivity—and thereby draw in positive experiences—or do you want to charge it with negativity, and bring in negative experiences?

Feeling bad is rough enough, but the worst part about feeling bad is that it perpetuates itself! If you need more motivation to move out of your bad and sad moods, that's it right there!

There are always going to be moments that throw you off your frequency, some little, like a bad driver, and some big, like the death of someone you love.

This is normal, it is human, and it is all part of the contrast of life which then inspires us to dream bigger and get clearer about what it is we want. As you can see, pain and contrast is actually essential in helping us grow and evolve, even though it can suck in the moment.

Allow yourself to experience your emotions at full capacity, yes, absolutely. But don't dwell on your pain, or make excuses to wallow in misery or self-pity. We could make excuses all day long as to why we are entitled to feel bad about this or that, and many of us do! However, I want to encourage you to remember that digging a deeper trench in the feeling bad place will never allow you to feel better. Why not just drop it and choose to feel good?

Make feeling good your number one priority. Make it the wish on every birthday candle you blow out. Make it your New Year's resolution in perpetuity. Once you begin to make feeling good your priority, you will notice that everything around you begins to change. It is like knocking down the first domino. The effects of this simple shift in thinking—and in turn, action—will be profound. The people with miserable attitudes will begin to melt away from you. The momentum will build. The next right action will become obvious, because it will follow inspired thought. And so on, and so forth.

Abraham-Hicks calls this feeling good stuff "being in the vortex." You are in the vortex any time you feel good and you're in the present moment. When the momentum is building and life has more color. When beautiful things just seem to happen. I know I am in the vortex when I find pennies on the ground, when I notice repeating numbers (also known as "angel numbers"), when I hit all the green lights and get the easy parking spaces, when people compliment me on my outfit or strike up a conversation in the street, when people give me things for free, when I get a table in a packed restaurant, when someone texts or calls just as I am thinking of them, when my friend and I say the same thing at the same time, and the list goes on. As you can tell, it is a wonderful place to be. Literally nothing feels better.

It's so easy to get there, too! Become aware of your moods. Remember that they are a *choice* (and that the longer you stay in a bad mood, the more you'll attract things of a similar vibration). Do something to change it by using your physical body. And then, simply continue to reach for a better feeling thought.

You've got this, baby. It's in the bag!

THE SECRETS OF SABOTAGE IN YOUR SUBCONSCIOUS MIND

Let's go a little bit deeper. What do you do about the times when feeling good seems almost impossible? What do you do when, despite your best efforts, you cannot seem to make a change in your life?

I'm going to introduce you to the idea of secondary benefits. This concept blew my mind when I first learned about it, and I hope it will do the same for you. Secondary benefits are the things we *gain*—usually at a subconscious level—from our undesirable behavior.

Let's use health and fitness as an example, because it is such a pertinent thing for so many of us. You may look at yourself in the mirror and feel dissatisfied, or eat a meal of fast food and feel awful, totally bloated and miserable. You think to yourself, 'I have to get to the gym and eat properly.'

But the next day, you skip the gym. You order another greasy meal. And the cycle continues.

Why does this happen when you know what you want and you know what you need to do?

From Google: Secondary benefits are "advantages which people often derive or receive from their physical, neurotic, and character disorders as well as life difficulties. It is theorized that the individual does not consciously and intentionally search for these benefits, but that there is a payoff (i.e., some enjoyment) in them."

Excuse the scientific terminology, but I really want you to understand this! In short, a secondary benefit is something you don't consciously desire, but that you derive enjoyment from.

In the case of neglecting your health, there are many secondary benefits that might be running the show.

Maybe you like the attention you get from complaining about how you look. Maybe talking about your weight or health is a way that you bond with others. (You may fear that without this topic of conversation, your friendships would dissolve.) Maybe your family has unhealthy eating habits too, and to buck the trend would change your relationships with them, or change the level of love and acceptance you feel from them. Maybe changing your own habits would make your loved ones feel bad about themselves, and you don't want to rock the boat that way. Maybe overeating allows you to numb out some feelings you'd rather not feel. Maybe it justifies a belief you have about yourself. Maybe it allows you to punish yourself in some way, thereby achieving a sense of relief from real or imagined guilt or shame.

This is big. These are heavy concepts. These are ways that we self-sabotage *without even knowing it.*

If you have trouble saving money, finding healthy relationships or anything else, ask yourself, 'What are the secondary benefits I am gaining from continuing to do this?'

If it's hard for you to save your coins, some of the secondary benefits might include not wanting to do better than your parents, friends, or peers (which dovetails with a fear of being cast out or ostracized); wanting the adrenaline rush of buying things (also a way of avoiding those pesky emotions!); or perhaps reinforcing a belief that you're not worthy of good things.

If you keep enrolling in shitty relationships, some of the secondary benefits might include having something to talk about, or using drama to get attention. It could be a form of self-punishment which gives you some slight relief. It may be reinforcing your belief that you're not good enough. You might be degrading yourself as a reenactment of childhood trauma. Or it might be a way to score the adrenaline rush of being constantly embroiled in drama.

If you can't quit smoking, maybe it is because it gives you a sense of connection to someone you love. If you keep cheating, maybe it is because you want attention and an adrenaline rush and you're punishing yourself.

...And the list goes on. Pretty wild, huh?

The thing is, there are always other ways to meet these secondary benefits. We can experience connection and get attention in healthier ways. There are thousands of ways to spike your adrenaline that do not require you to ultimately degrade yourself or hurt others. And there are ways to relieve yourself of guilt that do not include self-punishment.

We all hold onto bad habits and indulge our secondary benefits to some degree, and as you can see, it's largely unconscious. But now that you know that this is something you've been conditioned for, it is also something you can decondition. It is something you can change. And that's a beautiful thing.

IT'S NOT ABOUT A HABIT, IT'S ABOUT WHO YOU ARE

When we want to make some kind of change in our lives, we often make the mistake of simply trying to institute some new behavior. The problem is that *this new behavior or habit or routine we want to implement is at odds with how we actually see ourselves.* It clashes with the subconscious program we've been running our entire lives.

We are starting at the wrong end of the stick: with behavior, when we don't have a belief that backs it up. We actually need to change our beliefs first—once we do that, making a behavioral shift is easy!

I used to hate working out. Even the idea of it made me want to die. When I thought about it, I either associated it with being freezing cold in a frosty grass field in New Zealand, wheezing asthmatically, or punishing myself on the treadmill when I had an eating disorder. I had no positive associations with exercise. To me, it had always been a torture device. So when I turned 25 and decided—after moving into a fifth floor walk-up building in New York City that left me breathless every time—that I needed to get fit, getting myself to the gym was a major hurdle. Even though I had picked a cool gym, I always felt out of place there. I didn't feel stylish or cool or coordinated. In fact, I felt the polar opposite. My internal stories all swirled around the idea that I wasn't fit, I wasn't athletic, I wasn't coordinated, and I didn't belong there. I was an outsider.

These were all secondary benefits. By feeling like an outsider, I got to feel "special" and different. It fed my ego. By claiming that I wasn't athletic, I got to be lazy (which, let's face it, can feel great in small doses). And by refusing to work out, I was punishing myself, subconsciously—because exercise makes us look and feel good.

This programming was running my life. It was so uncomfortable to go to the gym. I would eye the treadmills and feel awkward, like I was fooling myself, like I would never be friendly with anyone there. It was really painful!

Everything changed for me when I started to *shift how I saw myself*. The best part is that it was really as easy as telling myself—and other people—a new story. After some floundering, I decided to hire a personal trainer, and we scheduled three sessions a week onto the calendar. I had never really worked out properly before, and I felt completely unsure of what I was supposed to. The expense felt absolutely astronomical, so I went to every single session, because I couldn't bear to waste the money!

Very quickly, I had to rearrange my life so that there was room within it for me to exercise. I started to wear my workout clothes more regularly, because I knew that three out of my five work days would end in the gym. I started to eat less processed food—especially those delicious spicy fried chicken sandwiches they sold at the bodega under my apartment—because I noticed that having a bunch of grease and gluten sloshing around inside me made my next workout so much harder. And when I would see my friends, I would sometimes end our lunches by heading to the gym. They would almost always ask me how it was going, and I would tell them that even though it was tough, I was enjoying it, and that I was going three times a week.

This is such a simple and subtle shift. The place where a lot of people falter is that they tell a story that is already unsuccessful. They may say something like, "I'm *trying* to get fit" or "I go to the gym when I can." Those were not my stories. My workouts were permanently embedded into my Google Calendar, honey! It began to change my perception of myself. And as I realized I was wearing gym gear a lot, I started to pay more attention to it. I began to put together gym "looks" and it made me feel better about going. The more I went to the gym, the more I got to know the staff and the trainers. I started to feel like I belonged. My trainer and I became friends and I looked forward to seeing him. And I started to think of myself as a "gym bunny"—which was a fun identity to slide into!

When something becomes your identity, it is much easier to implement and integrate new behaviors. Be sure to check the Book Bonuses section on galadarling.com for a guided tapping session on identity change! We are going to make this concept of feeling good part of your identity and lifestyle, rather than just a habit you want to get into.

What I want to encourage you to do is step into a whole new belief system. The belief that you are a strong, smart, positive babe. That you do things that make you feel good about yourself. That you look after yourself. That you make feeling good a priority every single day. Because that is all that this requires: just a little shift in perception. A little change in how you see yourself. It's so easy to do.

What this also means is that you stop telling yourself the stories that are holding you back and disempowering you. A lot of us make excuses. We tell ourselves—and the people around us—a sad story about our childhood (or even adulthood!) These stories are loaded with *secondary benefits*, allowing us to gain attention or sympathy, and sometimes these stories even manipulate other people into allowing us to get away with really unscrupulous behavior!

This is not to say that terrible things haven't happened to you. We *all* have experienced some kind of trauma, pain, maybe even abuse. My heart goes out to you because I know how hard that can be. But I also don't want you to latch onto the worst moments from your past and use them to create your identity. You are so much more than what has happened to you.

Some of the most successful people in the world came from horrific upbringings, full of abuse and pain. They have not allowed their past to dictate their present. In fact, sometimes they have even used those experiences to motivate them to be more, give more, help more. They have transformed their pain into purpose, and they have not allowed these secondary benefits to run their lives.

When we tell sad stories, we cement them even further into our consciousness. We are deepening that trench, digging the neural pathway deeper and stronger. What we are really doing is telling the story of "why I cannot be happy now"— and it is nonsense. You are so much more than your history! The best way to let go of these old stories is simple: never tell them again. Do not talk about anything that you do not want to further entrench in your life.

This means that we do *not* tell our stories of betrayal. We do not use the tale of tormented love as a cocktail party anecdote. We do not use the sad story to get attention, or to let ourselves off the hook for doing the work. This can be challenging... Especially those past incidents have coiled up inside you and turned into a major part of your identity. Just like all things in life, using pain and trauma as your identity is a *choice*.

Depression, anorexia, and anxiety used to be my identity. They were my "artistic fuel". I believed that I needed to be in pain to create. I would look at the artists I admired and observe their alcoholism, womanizing, pessimism, and think, 'That is the way to be a true creative. When your life is in shambles, you will make real art!'

Oh, the folly of youth!

My path to healing was not a glamorous one. I was essentially dragged there kicking and screaming. My ex-boyfriend threatened me that if I didn't work on myself, he would leave me. At the time, I valued my relationship more than I valued myself... So I did what he said.

It sounds completely nuts to write these words, but at the time, I didn't really want to be happy. I thought only stupid people could enjoy life, because all I saw was pain and misery. I was a professional cynic. And maybe the truth is that I was filled with so much self-loathing, anger and sadness that I didn't think I *deserved* happiness.

But once I discovered tapping at age 23, my depression was cured and as a result, my whole perception of the world flipped. I saw how beautiful the world could be. I realized that, actually, taking a cynical and negative view of things was simply laziness. It was easy to point at what wasn't working, be skeptical, and complain. It took skill and a disciplined mind to truly realize that *the world is what you make of it*, and even though there are things in life that we may not be thrilled about, there are also blessings everywhere. Choosing to put your attention on the things that make you feel good is a sign of strength, acuity, grit and resilience.

I thought it was clever to be miserable and cynical, that only the razor-sharp intellects of the world could see how terrible life truly was. I thought that if you were happy, you were clearly dumb and oblivious. But it turned out to be the exact opposite.

Next time you're in a public place, like the supermarket, or at the bus stop, listen to what the people around you are talking about. The law of averages tells us that most of these people will be of standard intelligence. And you will notice that almost all of them are complaining about something-or-other... Almost without exception!

Are these people experiencing bliss on a regular basis? Or are they average Joes, trapped in a life of their own miserable making?

Is this how we want to spend our lives, these precious hours in the Universe? Moaning and whining about things that are done and dusted? Do we really want to devote hours to dwelling on things that we can no longer change? I vote that we dig deep into the moment and extract every ounce of joy out of it. I vote that we fix our gaze on the horizon, and get absolutely *hyped* on the possibilities of the future. Screw the past. It's over. The time is now!

This is not a question of IQ. We all know geniuses whose lives are absolute misery in motion. It's not about being clever. This is about recognizing what works for us and then committing to it. It's about noticing what PROPELS us forward (hint: good feelings!) and then doubling down on them!

Some people think that they need to block out their emotions in order to get things done. This is one tactic, for sure. You'll probably be productive. But the problem is that if you stop paying attention to how you feel, you won't know whether you're doing the right thing or not... Because the right thing feels like a breath of fresh air, and the wrong thing feels like pushing a boulder up a hill. It's that simple. If you've decided to turn off your emotions, you will no longer be able to discern if what you are doing is helping or hindering you.

I remember once observing a boyfriend who was going through a stressful time at work. He decided that the best strategy was to shut down his feelings and push on through. He was tirelessly grinding from morning to night. He became very hard to talk to or connect with, because he was completely emotionally bereft. As this continued, he neglected his daughter's emotional needs, causing more problems. He sabotaged his relationship with me, got kicked out of his place of work, and lost tons of clients.

What would have been a better strategy?

What if, instead of obsessing about money and status, he had asked himself, "What do I need to do to FEEL GOOD every day? How can I encourage my clients to do the same? How can I bring more *joy* to my work? How can I make my clients' experience more fun?"

These ideas can seem antithetical, particularly when we're stressed out about money. It can seem like the only thing to do is get really serious, make a plan, and execute it. No time for any funny business! But actually, when we make joy and happiness priorities in our lives, everything is easier. We come up with more ideas. We are less stressed out. And we make real, lasting connections with good, authentic people.

When you are not letting yourself feel your true emotions, when you won't even admit them to yourself, you are also not letting anyone else really see you or know you. It becomes a very lonely life, because deep down, you know that you're hiding a big chunk of your truth.

The truth is that people want to be around other people that are real, that can be vulnerable, and who feel good. Even if you plaster a fake grin on your face, people know when you're not truly connected to yourself. It makes them uncomfortable... And so they go away.

We always attract what we are radiating. So if you are giving off a vibe of stress and seriousness and "hustle"—you will only attract yuckyness: people who are peddling "get rich quick" schemes, social climbers, business plans with no integrity, and other kinds of messiness.

Next time you are feeling stressed out about something, stop writing to do lists. Make a decision to get out of your *head* and into your *body*. Ask yourself, 'What can I do to feel a little relief? What can I do right now that will make me feel better?' It could be as simple as calling your BFF, it could be listening to your favorite album, it could be going to therapy or doing some tapping.

The goal is to always move yourself closer to relief, closer to satisfaction, closer to feeling good. When we change our state to one that is higher up the emotional scale, we stumble upon solutions. We have brilliant ideas. No one ever solved a problem by diving deep into a fear spiral, or by neglecting their emotional health. You cannot resolve an issue from the same consciousness that created the problem, which is why when Einstein was stuck on a tricky problem, he'd go away and eat an orange or play the violin.

Feel good FIRST, solve problems SECOND!

MASTERING THE BAD BITCH MINDSET

Calling all bondage babes! Have you ever been drawn to the kinky side? Ever slid your hands along a pair of PVC pants, dared to try on a spiked choker, or poked your head into the darkened door of a goth club?

What I want to encourage is for you to bring this vibe to your MENTALITY. Get kinky with it! Discipline your mind like a bad bitch!

Making feeling good your priority might sound like a hippy idea, but it is the exact opposite. It actually requires a finely-honed mind. It is a mental bootcamp. I've always loved those TV shows about people training to get into the military or whatever, even though I am no way inclined to do it myself. There's something about mental discipline and toughness that is really hot.

Having self-control is exciting. Being a person that has it together, doesn't make excuses, and maintains a positive attitude is sexy. Who doesn't want to be around that person? Scratch that—who doesn't want to be that person?!

When you notice that you are going down a spiral, just say to yourself, "Hey! No thanks." Let your negative thought know that you see it for what it is: an attempt to derail you from feeling good. When you shine your torch on it, it becomes less of a subtle manipulator and starts to look a bit pathetic. Look at it there, cowering in the corner. Who could really be afraid of that?

It really is that simple. We start with awareness: noticing that our mind is taking us to a dark or unpleasant place. Awareness is half the battle! Once you've noticed what is going on, you have the choice to stop your mind in its tracks or let it continue taking you deeper and deeper. The more that you do this, the less tolerance you will have for those unhappy thoughts, and the sooner you will course-correct.

This is a practice. It is something that you decide to start doing, and then maintain. In a similar way to how you are working gratitude and Magical Morning Practice into your life, you can add this too. You won't catch every single negative thought immediately, some of them will get by you. But the more of them you catch, the more you will be in control of how you feel.

When you team this mental practice with the tapping sessions in the Book Bonuses section, you will be absolutely floored by the speed with which you make progress!

LETTING GO OF CONDITIONAL HAPPINESS

Sure, it's easy to be happy when you get a text message from your crush, or you get a raise at work, or you're snuggled up on the couch with a pint of vegan chocolate ice-cream, watching your favorite trashy reality TV show.

It's so easy to allow an external circumstance to make us happy, but what if you try to be happy without those things? What if you decide to generate joy on your own?

The way that we can be happy without having to have our conditions met is by pre-paving the way. For example, if you wake up and immediately focus on something that doesn't feel good, then go on to have a series of aggravating interactions with people and don't hear from your lover all day, there's very little you can do to turn that all around. By the end of the day, you have so much momentum built up in a negative direction that you'd have to work your ass off to change it. That's why a morning practice is so important, and it's why I started doing the Magical Morning routine every day. It helps me to reach for satisfying thoughts and then the momentum of me having done that helps me to create a happier and more joyful day.

When we allow other people to dictate how we feel—which is exactly what happens when we don't pre-pave our day—we are not in control of our own vibration, and thus, we feel like we're just reacting most of the time. Think about the people you know who spend huge swathes of time complaining about their partner, family, colleagues or friends. What is really happening in this situation is that they are not taking responsibility for their own vibration. If you find yourself living amongst people who do not feel in alignment with what you want or value, be aware that complaining isn't going to make a lick of difference. If you are in this situation, either change it, or get so high on your supply (aka so deeply tuned into your own vibration) that it no longer bothers you.

When we're not conscious of the stories we're telling ourselves, and we're behaving in an unaware way, we find ourselves doing things that wound or hurt us. We get a little seedling of a negative thought in our minds, and we water it, tend to it, and nurture it until it becomes a huge tree. The truth is that we get to choose our thoughts, and so—plot twist!—we also get to ignore, avoid, or distract ourselves from the thoughts that bring us harm.

How often do you ask questions whose answers you already know are going to create more dread and fear within you? How often do you switch browser tabs, knowing that the thing you're about to type into the search box isn't going to make you feel good? How often do you allow a little kernel of curiosity to pop into a huge, anxiety-inducing piece of popcorn?

Newsflash: you don't have to do this! It is optional!

This is a mental discipline, as I keep saying. Don't feel bad as you think back on the million plus times you have done exactly these things, because you're not alone: I have done the same. It's not our fault. We didn't know better. We didn't know we could choose different thoughts. But here's the kicker: now we know. So we can make different choices. And that's where the growth and development happens!

HOW DO I KNOW THAT MY MANIFESTATIONS ARE WORKING?

This is almost a trick question, but I'll answer it! Remember at the start of the chapter where I told you that when you ask, it is given? There are no exceptions to this rule. That is what happens every single time. And remember when I shared Terri's brilliant UPS truck analogy? Same deal. *It is on the way.*

When you're feeling doubtful about your manifestations, think back to Chapter One where we talked about our emotions being our guidance. If you're feeling good, you will manifest more quickly. It is truly as simple as that!

So, your manifestations are always working. But if feeling good is not enough and you want to ramp it up to a supersonic level, I find the following to be massively positive signs. They always cheer me up and help bring me even further into alignment—bonus!

- ♥ Pennies on the ground. One is beautiful, and if I find two in a day, I know my vibe is LIT!
- ♥ Butterflies, especially blue or monarch butterflies
- ♥ Dragonflies, hummingbirds, and fireflies—these are all miracle creatures in my mind
- ♥ Pink anything: a fence, a building, a garbage truck (I saw a pink garbage truck today!)
- ♥ Spontaneous rainbows
- ♥ Repeating numbers, also known as angel numbers:

- 111 says keep going, you are on the right path
- 222 says you are in the right place at the right time, this moment is perfect
- 333 says balance your mind, body and spirit
- 444 says you are protected and guided.
- 555 says a change is happening
- 666 says step back and take a greater view
- 777 says you are stronger than you know, have faith
- 888 says you are perfectly balanced and in harmony
- 999 says it is time to wrap up the old and begin the new

I asked y'all on Instagram about signs that your manifestations were coming, and some of my favorite answers included balloons, planes, chimes, feathers, ladybugs, four-leaf clovers (someone found 84 in one year!), and white rabbits!

CAN LIFE REALLY BE THAT GOOD?

I believe that life can be sensational if we will allow it to be that way. But it is essential that we examine the subconscious programming that is underpinning our lives. This means that we need to take a real look in the mirror and see where we are letting ourselves down.

Gratitude lists, tapping, meditation, exercise and visualization are incredible tools but if, underneath it all, we are allowing our sense of self-loathing to rule the roost, we will never make as much progress as we want to.

I strongly encourage you to look at the areas of your life you'd like to change and ask yourself, 'What are the secondary benefits from me *staying the same?'*

Even though these can be uncomfortable questions to ask and difficult truths to face, the clarity you gain will be absolutely worth it.

Once you look into these things and realize where you have been holding yourself back, you will be unrestricted in the pursuit of truly feeling good. It will become even easier to align with the things you desire. Getting into the vortex every day will become second nature... And the life you dream about will come rushing towards you! ✳

"Step 1. Contrast helps you to define
what you want. Wanting is born out of it.
Clarity of desire." —Abraham-Hicks

03

STEP 1: CONTRAST (OR: THE GIFTS OF PAIN)

WAKE UP IN VENICE, ITALY, ONE OF THE MOST BEAUTIFUL AND surreal places on the planet. I stick my arm out from beneath a feathery duvet, pick up my phone, I look at my notifications, and feel that feeling: Lack. Scarcity. It grips me in the bottom of my heart.

Abraham-Hicks talks about "Step 1 moments." I am in one.

I want something that I don't have right now. Even though I feel gratitude, I am excited to be in Venice, and I am having a good time, I still feel lack. I still have wanting. I'm still lusting after something that has not yet physically manifested.

But what if the pain was a new mail notification, and the message is from the Universe?

The email might read as follows:

From: The Universe
To: Me
Time: 11:11am

Hi beautiful.

I noticed that you are feeling pain.

Here are some things that you should know about that.

Right now, you are feeling pain because you are focusing on the wrong things. You are looking outside of yourself to feel good. You are looking for love in all the wrong places. You are expecting outside conditions to make you happy, and putting the cart before the horse. You think that when you get this or that thing, you will feel happy, but that is not how it works. You need to feel good in order to bring what you want to fruition!

Feeling like this is an indicator that you need to get back into alignment with yourself. Notice how you are feeling, and then use it as fuel to get back on track. Okay?

The second thing about this pain you are feeling—which in this case we could also call yearning—is that it shows us that you are creating a big, hot ass desire. Your wanting proves that you are alive, that you are still in the journey of co-creating your life with the universe. If you didn't want anything, you'd be dead. Those little impulses you feel, whether it's wanting a fabulous holiday or a delicious new love, are all driving you forward. This wanting will allow you to fulfill what is in your vortex.

Don't feel bad about feeling bad. This pain is part of the process. Trust. It is all coming together beautifully.

But in the meantime… Why not do what you need to do to feel good? Allow those positive feelings to put this pain out of business. And just relax, because something even better is on its way.

Xo,

The Universe.

I lay in bed in Venice, contemplating these things. I decided to shift myself out of feeling bad by taking control of my vibration. So I got out of bed before anyone else was awake, meditated for 10 minutes, made myself a strong-ass espresso and then drank it while stretching on the floor and listening to Abraham-Hicks.

You may be wondering, 'What happened next?'

I had one of the best days of my entire trip, because I had set up my vibration early on. Did all my pain and anguish completely disappear? No. There was still a little bit of pain there, but it was okay because I was paying *more* attention to what felt good. (And I was wearing sequin pants, which definitely helped!)

Over the next week or so, my levels of joy fluctuated. I went up and came down again. I still had an awareness of the things that I wanted but didn't have at the moment. And while I was tempted to feel bad about feeling bad, it was important for me to rest in the knowledge that this is all part of the process.

It is, in fact, these moments of discomfort that propel us into a new manifestation. If you are not riding high right now, and if you are not in the vortex right now, that does not mean you are a bad person! You are not a bad person, you are not failing, you are not ruining your manifestations. You are creating new universes for yourself. It's perfect! You're perfect! You are in the exact right moment for you right now. **You are doing it exactly as you are supposed to.**

Being in this pain—which really is just the knowledge that there is something we want and do not have in physical manifested reality yet—shows us that we are in a STEP 1 MOMENT. We do not need to feel guilty for not wanting to poop a rainbow right here and right now! We are perfectly where we need to be: we are in a state of DESIRE, of wanting, of BEING ALIVE.

This is life. It has its ups and downs, and it is also *driven* by desire! This is what keeps us alive: wanting the next thing, letting the fever pull you forward into a new reality, and allowing it to pick up speed so that you can create a whole new world.

Now, there is the tricky part, and the part that most people don't tell you. **Desire is the whole point.** The actual obtaining of the thing provides only a short-lived joy.

As you know, feeling good is everything. Even though you may have a "real job," you know by now that your *most important job* is to do what it takes to feel good. It's about *alignment with ourselves*, and the fantastic thing is that this is such easy work to do! You can get yourself into alignment every day. It works. It is simple. It feels so satisfying, and it doesn't even take very long! In fact, the more practiced you are at this work, the sooner you can snap to alignment. You can do it in a few seconds. Whenever you feel off, you can notice and bring yourself back... Trivially! Just like I did in Venice!

Feeling good is the start of everything you want. Once you feel good, you can buy things, start projects, fill your closet, create relationships, write books, make TV shows, and do all the things that normal people think are going to make them happy. Spoiler alert: all the Ferraris in the world won't mean a goddamn thing if you are not in alignment. But there is so much joy to be had in letting desire move you, and then watching it come to fulfillment!

It is never about the *thing* that we want. It is about how we think that thing will make us feel. So we set off on an adventure to manifest something, never realizing that it is *who we become on the journey* that is what matters!

Think of life as a sexy eight lane highway. The whole purpose of this highway is to feel good. Keep driving, keep feeling good. Yum. Ever forward. And all the things we want—relationships, cash, a good reputation, a beautiful home—are like gas stations along the way. They are just little pit-stops, where you can stretch your legs and experience some relief and have a moment to reflect on how far you've come. *But they are not the point.* They are not the destination. They are just little dots along the way. The way you transform on the trip is the most beautiful part!

Some people find this hard to believe, but it's true. I have met and talked to so many people who have lived at such a high level—gained such fame, financial success, have homes full of beautiful things—who say that *it means nothing because they were unhappy.*

Hint: "Unhappy" is just code for "not aligned."

If you think Hollywood is full of people who are living their dream, you are right. But if you think that living your dream leads to unbridled joy, you are wrong.

Getting everything you want doesn't mean that you are happy. In fact, sometimes it only serves to prove that those things don't mean anything. Then you are really in a hot mess! You are no longer chasing things, because you now know that "things" don't work. Now you have to start the work on getting aligned with who you are.

Even Kylie Jenner knows this! In episode one of her reality show, *The Life Of Kylie*, she said, "The only different thing about me, or out of the ordinary, really, is probably just that I have nice things. But what you realize when you get there—when I know I could buy any car, any house—is that that *happiness lasts two seconds.* That's not my real happiness, that's not where I find happiness. I'm so blessed that I got to experience this at such a young age and learn that, so now I can find what really is going to make me happy."

A quote like that might make you want to tear out your hair, when you think about the fact that she was worth a billion dollars at about 20 years old. But really, she's not saying that to stir the pot. She's expressing a truth that *many* of us will never *actually* fully understand or be able to integrate into our lives. If we pay attention, we can avoid making the attainment of stuff central to our lives.

Russell Brand has said something similar. "I know change is possible, I know there is an alternative because I live a completely different life to the one I was born with. I also know that the solution is not fame or money or any transient adornment of the individual. The only revolution that can really change the world is the one in your own consciousness, and mine has already begun. The more that I've detached myself from the things that I thought would make me happy like money and fame and other people's opinions, the more truth is being revealed."

Again, this can be frustrating to hear, because so many of us spend our entire lives chasing the things that people like Kylie Jenner or Russell Brand broadcast to the world. We all want to be beautiful and adored and successful and drive a nice car! But let's just step back and be objective about it. If the people who have everything we've ever dreamed of are *still not satisfied*, maybe we can see them as cautionary tales and really *pay attention* to what they're saying. Because even though these people may have "more" on the outside than we do, they are not any different from you or me.

This is where navigating life can sometimes get tricky. We do not want to be constantly chasing the next thing and expecting this next one to make us happy. It doesn't work like that, but it can be a very easy place to get stuck.

I watched a documentary called *Generation Wealth* recently which very accurately documented the downfalls of this kind of pursuit.

A man, who was a former hedge fund manager, now on the run from the FBI, was telling a story about sitting in a bay with his wife. They were having dinner at a restaurant, looking out at the super-yachts docked nearby. Each was worth several million dollars. He was pointing at them, asking her, "Which one do you want? This one? That one?" Her reply—which made him cry as he recounted it—was, "I don't want a boat. I just want you to put your phone down."

You will not be surprised to hear that, in addition to (eventually) losing his fortune, he also lost his wife and children.

Now obviously, this is an extreme case. And perhaps I am being a little heavy-handed with the examples... But they are important. And maybe it is confusing or weird to have some cautionary tales about getting everything that you want in a book about manifesting!

My intention is not to turn you off of wanting lovely things, experiences, and people in your life. Absolutely, you should have all of those things and so much more! I believe that everyone should have everything they want, and they can. Bringing our dreams to fruition is one of life's great delights and it is part of the deal of being alive! But it's the *bringing* that is more satisfying than the fruition. And it would be inaccurate for me to portray the pursuit of anything external as being the "purpose of life," because we all know that it isn't.

You have had this experience yourself, I know it. You're in a store and you're salivating over this or that object. My friend Mystic Medusa calls this "thing-lust." Thing-lust is real! Thing-lust feels *amazing*. It happens to me most frequently when I walk into a big department store, which is like kryptonite to me. Crystal-covered stilettos, a purple cape, eccentric sunglasses, oversized hats in every color... It whips me into a frenzy. I just love taking it all in, especially with a friend, so we can sniff perfume, touch fabrics, and ooh and aah over all the lovely objects!

Once I find a thing I want, the excitement reaches a fever pitch. I deliberate over it in my mind. I ask myself questions like: Do I really want it? What will I wear it with? Is this a practical purchase? (Answers: Yes! Who knows! Definitely not!) And once I finally decide to pull the trigger... It is a raging crescendo of joy. They wrap up whatever it is. I hand over my card. I leave with a shopping bag. I am excited for about 30 more seconds. And then... ? I walk to my car. I start texting someone. I choose a playlist. I wonder about what I'm going to do tonight.

Things are FUN but it's the actual build up that is the most thrilling part for many of us! Once we have the item at home, nestled on a shelf or displayed on a tabletop, it's still lovely, but it's no longer an item that drives us wild or has us frothing at the mouth.

The thrill of the chase is so built into our biology that we are almost powerless to resist it, so we need to be *aware of it*. Have you ever had the experience of being obsessed with a love interest... *Until* they confirm that they want you too? Then you're like, 'Hmmm. Do I really wanna do this?'

Once upon a time, a man I thought was pure magic told me he loved me. We'd been building to that point for a while. In fact, that very day I had felt worried about whether he would ever say that at all. It felt like a major coup. So what did I do? I went out on a date with someone else that very night!

When my first book came out, I went to visit it at Barnes & Noble. It felt good for about five seconds, and then it felt like *nothing*. It threw me into a total existential crisis. I thought, 'Oh my god. I have been working my whole life to publish a book, and now it's done, and I don't even care! It doesn't feel good or special or wonderful at all! What am I doing?! I'm wasting my life!'

About six months later, after much contemplation (and hand-wringing), I finally realized that the true joy of writing a book was in the writing of it: the research, putting the words together, those moments when the sentences thread together like silk, when you're in the flow and it just pours out of you. The joy was in signing the book deal. The joy was in meeting women and having them tell me how much it had meant to them. And of course, the joy was in how my life had evolved and shifted as a result of completing the project.

The number of examples I have of this pursuit-based obsession are almost non-stop. We have all heard a million times that it is not the destination but the *journey* that counts. And it's a cheesy old adage, but it is absolutely true.

If this chapter doesn't teach you anything else, please know that the obtaining of things is not the point. It is the joy of *getting there* that is most important. It is the PATH. That is where you will find excitement and satisfaction.

PAIN IS NOT YOUR MASTER, IT IS YOUR SERVANT

A common mistake we make is thinking that pain owns us. That it dominates us, rules us, controls us, and pushes us into doing things we don't want to do.

It's true that we can let pain take the lead. We can let our fears overtake us and call the shots. We can feel the knot in our stomach and decide to back away from that thing we want, allow our fretting over a response to stop us from saying what we really need, decide that we don't want to be criticized and keep playing small.

Pain is a shitty master. Letting pain rule your life will mean that you never reach for what you want, never let your authentic self out to play, never let people really know you for fear of reprisal. What a waste.

In the words of Missy Elliott, let's flip it and reverse it! How different would your life be if you chose to view pain as your servant, rather than your master? What if we used pain as a data source?

Pain is information. If you put your hand in a fire, yes, it hurts, but that quick sharp shock of pain is better than keeping your hand there, having your sweater catch a spark, and going up in flames. Emotional pain functions the same way: it is a system that lets us know what is going on inside of us.

Do you remember when I said in the last chapter that our emotions are an essential part of manifesting? This is why. We need to be dialed into how we feel—both the pleasure and the pain—to steer our own ship.

Experiencing pain doesn't mean you've made a mistake or that you've ruined something. It is simply information, and it is an ABSOLUTELY essential part of the manifesting process!

Without feeling pain, lack, scarcity, or fear, we would not know what we want. We would not be aware of what it is we desire. We would not be able to shoot rockets of desire and get to the next place in our lives. The feeling that something is not quite right, or not exactly how we would like them, is compulsory.

Think about all the times in your life when you have noticed an absence or wanted more than you had in that moment. While it may not have been pleasant to go through those emotions, they did help you get to the next level. They were essential in creating this reality that you live in now. They catapulted you to these present moment manifestations!

Feeling pain means that you are in a Step 1 moment, and if you weren't having them, you would be dead! Being in a Step 1 moment is essential and it happens to absolutely every single one of us, no matter how much you "have." It doesn't matter who you are, how fat your bank account, how lush your love life, or how good your health: there is always more to want.

And this is where we walk a delicate balance: the balance of striving and moving forward, while also not getting fixated upon those things we want.

(This is yet another reason why a Magical Morning Practice is important. When we take a moment to center ourselves, to remind ourselves of what we have that is already so good, to think about what we desire, we are able to understand our life with greater context. We are reminded of where we have come from and where we are going, and we can see the trajectory of our existence. It becomes less about grasping in the moment, and more about having a greater cosmic overview of the events that make up our journey.)

A Step 1 moment is the genesis of all creation. In a Step 1 moment, we ask for what we want. How do we do this? By feeling uncomfortable, or by feeling lack.

In an instance of contrast—where we are being presented with something we don't like—we experience desire. It happens without much conscious thought, it is an automatic response. You see something you don't feel good about and you *instantly* create a desire for something different.

This desire that you've conjured up is added to your vortex, and as soon as this happens, the Universe starts to pull together all the cooperative components to make it real.

So, to summarize: **if you didn't feel awful from time to time, you wouldn't be able to create amazing things in your life.** The moments of contrast are an ESSENTIAL part of the puzzle.

WHAT CAN I DO WITH ALL THIS PAIN?

"You have the opportunity to turn your pain into something beautiful. Get out of self-pity and get into life." —Dave Navarro

So we have acknowledged that pain is normal, and that we are going to feel it no matter who we are, and no matter what our life looks like. Great! Except... Just having this knowledge doesn't make it any easier to feel pain! Pain is painful!

Let's look at what we can do with it when it arises.

♥ DEAL WITH YOUR PAIN AS SOON AS YOU FEEL IT

I used to hold onto my pain in a weird combination of resistance and denial. It would pang me—because it always does—and I would swallow it and try to pretend it wasn't there. I would tell myself it was no big deal. I would logic it away. ("Other people have it worse!") I would keep quiet, and I'd try to push it away.

The problem is that what we resist persists. The pain would turn into resentment and anger, which I would carry around, letting it bubble away inside me. Eventually I would explode with it, and create even more problems. The longer you wait to address your issues, the harder they will be to deal with. Today, when I feel some pain, I deal with it as quickly as I can. Sometimes that means I have a conversation with someone, and sometimes it means I use one of the techniques below. It almost doesn't matter what you do, as long as you do something!

Nayyirah Waheed has a one-line poem which goes: "grieve. so that you can be free to feel something else."

Mmmm. Yes. That's what it's all about. Feel it—really allow yourself to feel the totality of the emotion—and give it space to move through you, so that you can feel something else.

♥ TAPPING

By now, you are well aware that tapping is my go-to technique when I am feeling out-of-sorts. You don't have to sit there in anxiety when you feel bad. And hopefully by now, through the Book Bonuses section, you have done enough tapping to realize that it almost doesn't matter what you say as long as you tap on the points and focus on how you're feeling!

The idea isn't necessarily to move from feeling bad to feeling ecstatic, although that can happen! All we want to do is let go of whatever is holding us down. There is no issue too seemingly minor: if you want to move away from it, you can.

In tapping, we move through a process of acknowledging and releasing our pain. We notice it, we become aware of it, we hone in on what it is actually about, and then we truly let it go. In letting it go, we affirm to ourselves that it is all okay. While we tap, we state that we love ourselves, forgive ourselves, accept ourselves as we are right now. Nothing is as powerful as that.

Tapping is also an incredible way of processing our side of the street. Sometimes our pain occurs as a side-effect of our relationships with other people, and even when we speak our piece, we don't always get the response or reaction that we want. So when we tap, we take full responsibility for what is going on with us.

Sometimes, just our own tapping can transform the energy of the relationship so much that we do end up getting the response we want, but we can never count on that. This is a process we do for our own peace, although of course an interpersonal shift can be a wonderful benefit!

If you'd like to learn more about tapping, I have endless resources for you! See galadarling.com for everything you need to know.

♥ FORGIVENESS

Another thing we can do with the pain we're feeling is forgive. With tapping, we forgive ourselves, which is a huge piece of the process. But when we actively practice forgiving other people, we are able to drop the bag of rocks that we are carrying. It lightens our hearts.

My friend Colin Bedell has a morning practice where he—in addition to reading and meditating—actively prays for the people he has conflict with. He prays that they are happy, healthy, and healing. This is a lovely thing to do, and if you're struggling with some of the people in your life, it is definitely worth a try.

The practice of forgiveness is not always perfect, and the pain or anger we feel over a situation may re-emerge, even if we make forgiveness a priority. But the very intention to forgive the people who have hurt us can make such a difference to the weight we are carrying around on a daily basis. Willingness creates miracles in our lives.

♥ WRITING IT DOWN

Another powerful technique we can use in order to let things go is to write them down. My favorite way to do it is write a letter that you will never send. When you do this, you are able to process your feelings and get things off your chest, without worrying about the response or the reaction. It is immensely freeing and liberating. I'm not the only person who does this, by the way... Obama was well-known for doing this exact thing during his presidency!

You may be tempted (for speed and efficiency purposes) to write on a computer, but it's even better to hand-write these letters. Slow down, take your time, and let yourself really feel it with a pen in your hand. Handwriting is a somatic experience, and since we store a lot of pain and trauma in our bodies, when we use our bodies in this way, we are helping ourselves heal.

Whichever way you do it, I recommend purging the writing once it is done. On an energetic level, I don't like to hold onto negative feelings, even if they are out of the body and onto the page. My favorite way to do this is to literally set it on fire! Fire has been used by humans to purge feelings for centuries, so why not?!

♥ VISUALIZE LETTING IT GO

Visualization is an inarguably effective way to change our lives, and it applies when it comes to feeling bad, too. I like to pair it with meditation. So, sit back or lie down, and then calm your mind. Focus on your breathing for a couple of minutes, and allow yourself to get really still.

Then, move into your ugly feelings—whatever they are—and let yourself picture them. We all picture things differently, so you might see it as a movie montage of moments, or as words written in the sky, or something else. Then, gather them all up and put them into a red balloon. Inflate the balloon, and imagine yourself walking with this balloon. In my mind, I like to walk to the end of a wharf on the water. Then, let the balloon go. Watch it fly up into the sky and keep watching until it completely disappears from view.

♥ HELP SOMEONE ELSE

To get out of pain, we always have the option of helping others. There are few better ways to stop indulging in our self-centered thoughts than by extending a hand to someone else!

In fact, this is a major part of the 12 Step recovery program (such as AA). We make ourselves available to others, we become a source of comfort for someone else who is in pain or is struggling, and we offer assistance wherever we can.

One of the reasons why I do the work I do is because it helps me stop focusing on my own pain! And I don't just do this online or in my books or with my clients. If I'm experiencing contrast, one of the first things I do is call a friend and ask about their life. Because believe me, you are not the only one who has issues or problems or complexities in their life. When you ask your friends what's going on with them, you are reminded that it's not just you. We are ALL going through something all the time!

When it comes to pain, we often think we are the only ones struggling. We think our difficulties are an isolated experience, and nothing could be further from the truth. We believe that we are the only people who have ever experienced unrequited love, or the death of a parent, or struggled with our finances. Literally all humans deal with these things, so reaching out and helping others process their own struggles assists them, lets them know they are not doing this alone, and reminds us that we are not alone either.

❤ NEVER TALK ABOUT IT AGAIN

This one is perhaps the most challenging aspect of letting go of our pain, especially in a world where we are encouraged to comb through our trauma in therapy for years and years. There is scientific evidence that every time you talk about an experience from the past, your body doesn't know the difference between a memory and the present moment—so you experience it all over again every time you talk about it.

Therapy has value, because it is important to understand your past, and why you do the things you do. Self-awareness is a major part of growth.

But once you understand what happened in your life, it is imperative to move forward with enthusiasm. You probably don't need to be in talk therapy forever, because it is of limited efficacy. Somatic treatments—therapies that are centered around the body, because this is where we store trauma—are very powerful in terms of healing old pain.

Still, we don't want to get stuck obsessing over ourselves. I see this a lot with people who are fixated on healing. There is a point where it becomes self-indulgent and an excuse for not choosing to feel good and move forward. It's so much healthier to simply accept yourself where you are, do the best you can and enjoy your life.

There is no healing session that will unlock absolutely everything and restore you to who you were as a pure little baby, innocent and untarnished. The point of life is not to undo all the things that were "done" to us. The point is to have FUN!

The more we talk about our pain, the more we ground ourselves in it and make it a part of our story, the more deeply we will experience it, and the more often we will attract similar moments that resonate with it. So let's make an effort to stop telling the painful stories, and instead talk about what is working, what makes us joyful, and what elevates us!

JUICY QUESTIONS CREATE JUICY ANSWERS

Here's a question to ask yourself: can you savor the problem as much as you savor the solution?

In other words, juicy questions (aka juicy problems) bring juicy answers (aka juicy solutions). The contrast is actually serving you, helping you experience more clarity, clearer asking, and a more delicious future.

When you view it this way, contrast doesn't seem so difficult. You can zoom out and realize that all these so-called problems are actually assisting you in creating a delicious life.

I STILL DON'T WANT TO FEEL PAIN

Fair enough. None of us do. But it is still an essential piece of the puzzle.

I would love to be able to tell you that if you do X, Y or Z, you will never experience pain or contrast again. Imagine how easy life would be! But would you really want that? Without those lows, the highs wouldn't feel like much at all.

On the other side of contraction is a massive expansion. No contraction? No expansion. Feeling pain and contrast and things we don't want to feel is like being in a meat tenderizer which softens us up so that more good can permeate through. Contraction makes a space for new, delightful things to enter our lives. If it didn't open you, there would be no space! So it is essential to feel the pain, not attach to it, and let it move.

HOW TO LET GO

It's important that we don't grip so tightly to life that we forget that we simply cannot control everything. Yes, there are things within our grasp, and then there are things which will always be outside of what we can change or improve. You cannot control whether a drunk driver is on the road at the same time you are. You cannot control the type of body you were born into. What I believe is that we have free will, which means that any circumstances that come our way, any hardships that befall us, we have the ability to play that hand with power. We can turn this pain into gold, into wisdom, into the life lessons that imbue our existence with greater meaning.

Our best antidote to gripping, grasping, and controlling life is to be in the present, and live each moment to our fullest capacity. When we truly understand that the contrast of pain or things we don't want is a gift, and that the Universe has a greater imagination then we ever will, we can relax. The twists and turns of our life create excitement and adventure, and that tension only serves to add to the richness of our lives.

If we can drop the urge to control everything around us, we will experience more peace, more joy, more harmony. We will feel good more often... And that's the whole point. ✳

04

STEP 2: CREATION

N THE LAST CHAPTER, WE DISCUSSED THE NECESSARY EXISTENCE of pain and how, even though no one enjoys it in the moment, it is an essential piece of our lives. As you cast an eye over your life, you will notice the things you don't like, and when you do this, you create desire.

Desire is instant. It shoots out of you, a firework that you cannot control. Desire is a kind of cosmic orgasm, created inside of you and released into the Universe in a shower of sparks.

As soon as a desire is born, its purpose is to bring itself into tangible reality. Imagine the Universe as the inside of a clock, all cranks and wheels and gears, infinitely turning and creating ever new things. It conjures up people, crafts experiences, and fabricates lovely things. It is always whirling and twirling and presenting to us if we can be open enough to notice it.

You have desires because you were meant to attain them.

Our desires are the genesis of all that is real. If we feel shame about them and try to suppress them, we twist inside and become bitter. People who do not honor their desires *loathe* those of us who do. They cannot be happy for others. They will do whatever it takes to tear us down, as if that is somehow the panacea for their despair. Sadly for them, this does not work!

If you decide to pay attention to your desires, you may struggle with believing firstly that they are possible, and secondly that you are deserving of them. It is hard for some of us to trust that *we really can have everything we want*, and that it is okay for us to have it.

We are raised to believe that hard work is everything, and that nothing good comes without a struggle (pro tip: sometimes the only struggle is allowing ourselves to have what we want!). We are told not to be greedy, that we are not special, that we should be satisfied with the mediocre types of lives that we see so many other people living.

And yet, these desires—to do and feel more, to be happier, to experience bigger and better things—are what propel us forward as a society. Desire drives science, exploration, and human achievement. Without it, we would be floating, aimless and goalless.

As Abraham-Hicks says, "The reason you want every single thing that you want is because you think you will feel really good when you get there. But if you don't feel really good on your way there, you can't get there. You have to be satisfied with *what is* while you're reaching for more."

The attainment of the desire is never the point. (Thinking that it is will only create suffering in your life.) But the journey towards the attainment of that desire is everything, and that's why it is so vitally important to learn how to be in the moment, and to enjoy it.

I am writing this while sitting in my garden, and as I type, I am vividly aware that this air I am breathing, the breeze I feel across my neck, the sun beaming down onto me, is where all the joy is. Just being here, pink bunny slippers on my feet, thinking and typing, this is the sweetest moment.

Every single moment of your life can be the best one if you are aware of it.

So the big question is: how do we sink into the moment, really and truly? How do we enjoy the process of manifesting without getting hung up on whether our manifestations are here yet or not? How do we enjoy our life as it is right now, without conditions?

That's what this next chapter is all about. I am going to walk you right through it. ✳

05

STEP 3: RELEASE AND ALLOW

Step 2: Creation is easy. It happens automatically, without any effort. Step 3: Release And Allow is where most people get stuck. But curiously, Step 3 also clicks into place when we stop efforting. When we stop trying. When we finally, finally, let go of the reins and just allow.

This can be one of the hardest things to do, especially for us closet control freaks!

We are all so different, and we all have different beliefs about life and how things come to us.

Some people believe that everything can come easily. They are relaxed, they enjoy the thrills of life, and they accept that the universe's timing is always divine and perfect. These are the blessed few, the ones people envy!

Other people believe that some things are easy to manifest, but some are more difficult. They always have a lover, but can never find a job. Or money flows, but their love life is a mess. It seems like as soon as they have one thing, another thing drops off. They are always juggling!

Finally, some people believe that *everything* is difficult to manifest! Nothing comes easily to these people! They believe suffering is essential, and even when they get something they want, they are always waiting for the other shoe to drop. Yes, that's right: even when they obtain some level of success, they cannot enjoy it because they are obsessed with the possible pitfalls. There is very little joy in life for these people. They will beat their heads against the wall for a very long time.

Who is right? Well, whatever you believe is right! Whatever you tell yourself will come true!

In truth, *none* of it is difficult. Nothing is hard to manifest. It is all the exact same thing! Bringing a desire to fruition is bringing a desire to fruition. Why would some things be easier than others in an infinite universe? The only reason why some things seem to be at arm's length is because of what you believe. The stories we tell ourselves are what make the difference!

The very first lesson in A Course In Miracles is, "There is no order of difficulty in miracles. One is not "harder" or "bigger" than another. They are all the same."

This step, Step 3, is about letting go. Trust is essential. Relaxation becomes a priority. Loosening the grip is everything.

When we don't do this, we find ourselves in a loop. We feel stress (which is really just fear and overwhelm). We obsess. We vibrate at a low frequency, which draws in similarly low frequency people and experiences.

It's really easy to stay stuck in a low vibration. As you now know, like attracts like. What this means is that a little bit of a bad feeling attracts more of the same. It grows and swells and gains momentum from there. Feeling bad begets feeling bad, so realistically, all you have to do is put your attention on it and allow it to grow! It's easy!

Interested in how not to do it? There are a multitude of things you can do to make sure your bad morning turns into a bad week, month, or year. Here's a helpful list to remind you!

HOW TO ENSURE THAT YOUR LIFE SUCKS

♥ KEEP TALKING ABOUT YOUR PROBLEMS

Pay a lot of attention to the things in your life that are not going well or are causing you a lot of pain. Look at what you dislike and make a big energetic ruckus. Notice it, focus on it, and talk to your friends about it. Complain loudly and vehemently! You could even come up with a little comedy routine about it, so that you are rewarded for your "funny" misery drill. Make a habit of pondering your problems first thing in the morning, and last thing before you go to bed. Allow yourself to dwell and wallow.

♥ BE SELF-CENTERED

This one is crucial. Make sure that you spend a lot of time thinking about yourself, and especially the many ways in which your needs are not getting met. Make your problems more important than other people's problems, and be sure to position yourself as a victim who others cannot possibly understand. Don't help others, never do anything unless you know you will get something back, and always be too proud and stubborn to accept outside assistance.

♥ DON'T DISRUPT YOUR NEGATIVE THOUGHTS

Let them lead you down the trail! If you want your life to suck, it is essential that you give your negative thoughts as much time as they ask for. Make sure you don't interrupt them by doing pesky things like tapping, dancing, helping others, creative projects, watching something that makes you laugh, practicing gratitude, or anything else that makes you feel good.

♥ IGNORE SPIRITUAL AND ENERGETIC PRACTICES

Just say no to looking after yourself. Refuse to take responsibility for your spiritual, energetic, and emotional health. Even though you know that you need spiritual and energetic practices, bury your head in the sand. Refuse to do them. Procrastinate like a pro! Come up with excuses as to why you shouldn't bother or don't have time. And for God's sake, don't do the Magical Morning Practice!

♥ SPEND TIME WITH MISERABLE PEOPLE

Only surround yourself with people who dwell in low vibrations. Invite them into your space and let them suck up your time with their negative energy and sad, disempowering stories. Ask for more details when something goes wrong. Never encourage them to reconsider the way they think about things. Allow their beliefs to color your beliefs. Spend a lot of time talking with them about the ways in which relationships, society, and life are all designed to make your life hard and unpleasant.

♥ PAY ATTENTION TO CRITICS

Put a lot of stock in what other people say, but particularly those who are professional critics or trolls. Few things will make you suffer more than listening to what people who have never achieved anything meaningful. If you look at someone's life and it is completely void of anything that inspires you, be sure to take whatever they say extremely personally, and then try to contort your life to make them happy!

♥ DON'T EXERCISE

God no. Why would you do that to yourself? Why would you want a strong heart, lungs and bones, clear arteries, lower blood sugar, a healthier weight, regulated blood pressure, or to prevent cancer? Why would you want to release endorphins—the "feel good" chemical—for free? No, no. Far better to drink, smoke, take drugs, shop, and eat sugar to try to feel better.

♥ SAY NO TO NEW OPPORTUNITIES

Whatever you do, don't take any risks. Play small and be afraid. Stay in your house and don't accept invitations. Don't try to push any boundaries or do things differently. It's important to stick to your routine, especially if it's so boring that you want to throw yourself out the window.

❤ SAY YES WITHOUT BOUNDARIES

...But be sure to make yourself overly emotionally available to people who have no qualms about demanding it. Run yourself ragged, helping them out, giving them a place to stay, cooking for them and cleaning up after them, accepting all kinds of crumbs, and then—this is essential—blame yourself for feeling resentful. This is the perfect cherry on top of a poisonous sundae! I told you it was easy! How many people do you know who are living their lives like this right now?!

GET OFF THE SUBJECT, SWEETHEART!

Learning to *allow* our blessings is a bit of a mental trick. It requires us to let go of the things we think we need, usually by changing our state or making ourselves think about something else. And when I say something else, I really mean ANYTHING but the thing you've been obsessing over!

You could think about your dog, your best friend, a trip that you want to go on, what you'll wear tomorrow, a shop you'd like to open... Anything! Ask your friends to help you think about other things! Keep yourself busy: pick a new project and throw yourself into it. Clean your house! It truly doesn't matter. You just want to keep your mind from going down that scarcity plughole.

TAP IT OUT

One of my favorite ways to release and allow is, you guessed it, tapping!

Last week I was talking to a friend about creating a tapping video to help people let go of whatever had happened the year before so that they could move forward into the new year feeling powerful and clear. She said, "Wow, that sounds amazing." She mentioned something that had happened to her that had caused her a lot of pain and self-doubt, and said, "Thinking about tapping on that makes tears come to my eyes. I've been to therapy and I know what it was about, but I'm still clearly hanging onto it."

"That's the thing about tapping," I said. "Therapy is amazing for understanding why, but tapping helps you excavate it entirely and remove it from your body. It's like pulling a bad tooth. Therapy helps you understand why it started to decay in the first place, but unless you get rid of it, it'll continue to rot."

Tapping is the perfect tool for getting your mind off the subject, taking the emotional charge out of it, and giving you a new sense of clarity so you can do something else with your time!

Any fear or sadness that you feel is resistance, and you can tap that out. When you remove the resistance, you will have movement!

MOVE YOUR BODY

Few things will get you into another zone like exercise. The real key to changing how you think about things—and how much you think about them in general—is to *change your state*. Moving your body is one of the fastest ways to do this!

I would go nuts without a physical outlet. When I am in the gym, or on the bike, or taking a walk, listening to a thumping playlist and pushing myself, I am able to get out of my head and into my body. We only suffer when we spend too much time in our minds thinking about ourselves and our problems. Give yourself the gift of freedom from your own thoughts!

HELP SOMEONE ELSE

Move away from your pain by reminding yourself that other people exist! Call or go and visit a friend, and instead of talking about your problems, get fully involved in what's up with *them*. What are they struggling with? How can you help them?

This will restore a sense of balance and perspective to your life, because no matter what you are going through—and no matter how you perceive your own "lack"—I promise that someone you love is going through something challenging too.

LEARN TO MASTER YOUR EMOTIONS

In order to master your emotions—aka calming yourself down and moving away from turbulent feelings—you should ensure you are addressing your physiology, your focus, and your language. Tony Robbins says that mastering these three things gives you greater control over how you are feeling, and he is right.

Your physiology is what you're doing with your body. Are you sitting up straight or are you slumped over? Are you eating good food and exercising or are you neglecting yourself?

Your focus is where you choose to put your attention. What are you thinking about? How did you set up your day? Did you do your Magical Morning Practice? Are you focusing on what's working in your life?

Your language is what you say—both to yourself and to the people around you. Are you using empowering language or are you casting yourself as a victim? Are you complaining or are you looking for solutions?

These are things we *inherently* know we should be paying attention to, but when we're in the throes of an intense feeling, it all goes out the window. Write "PHYSIOLOGY / FOCUS / LANGUAGE" on a Post-It and stick it on your wall!

THERE IS NO ISSUE WORTH SACRIFICING THE VORTEX FOR

When feeling good truly becomes your priority, you will begin to realize that there is simply no issue that is worth sacrificing the vortex (that feeling good place). Your tolerance for pain or thoughts of lack will get shorter and shorter, and soon you will be so committed to feeling good that you will do whatever it takes to navigate to a better-feeling thought.

Think of all those awkward family dinners you've sat through, especially those moments where a well-meaning relative starts to bring up something you just don't want to talk about. Do you remember how amazing your jiu jitsu skills have been in those moments? You took charge of that situation and steered everyone away from the topic like a professional! You dodged, bobbed, weaved, distracted, side-stepped... This is the exact same skill-set. Just don't let yourself go there, honey!

HOW LONG ARE YOU WILLING TO SUFFER?

One of my favorite ways to break away from thoughts of lack or focusing on what I don't have is by asking myself a very simple question: "How long am I willing to suffer over this?"

The answer, inevitably, is, "Oh! I'm not willing to suffer at all!"

The last time I asked myself this, I flashed back in time and realized I had been putting myself through pain for months. I had had enough. I didn't need a second serving of the pain parfait! I was full, thank you! That was the beginning of switching my thinking, and focusing on something else.

GET INTO THE VORTEX AND THEN...

We all know that we should look after ourselves and engage in self-care practices, but if we jump right into them without taking care of our frequency first, they won't feel very good. In fact, they might just make you mad.

The reason for this is it's very tough to move from furious to ecstatic bliss. They are several steps apart on the energetic ladder. We have to work our way there, incrementally.

So let's say you're having a tough morning. Things aren't feeling great. You feel like maybe you should say some affirmations, but the idea of doing it makes you want to roll your eyes so hard they'll get stuck in your head.

The trick is to work your way up the energetic scale first. Get into the vortex, and *then* do your self-care practices!

How do you get into the vortex? Change your state. Move your body! Tap, dance, sing, listen to a lecture, do a gratitude practice, take a walk, or engage in some combination that gets you there. Then, once you're in that good feeling place, make with the affirmations!

This completely changes how we do any self-care practice, because we're coming to it from a place of abundance, joy and overflow, rather than a place of lack, fear and uncertainty. You are gonna love this!

Years ago, I created a practice where I would have people make a list of their five biggest limiting beliefs. Then, on the other side of the paper, I'd have them create five affirmations to combat these beliefs, and have them tap them in every single morning! (You might say they're "tapfirmations"!) So if one of your limiting beliefs is that you're too weird to be lovable, the perfect antidote might be, "Weird people are my favorite type of people!" or, "My weirdness is my greatest asset!"

This exercise can be as unique as you, because we are all struggling with different things, and we all have different words that are meaningful to us.

For some of us, yelling, "I am the baddest bitch on the planet!" will rock our world.

For others, "I am exactly where I need to be" is the perfect revolution.

Some hints for coming up with your own tapfirmations:

♥ The goal of a tapfirmation is to deeply implant a new belief about yourself, so come up with something that feels resonant, exciting, and gives you a sense of internal strength, power, and joy!

♥ You can start the tapfirmation with "I am..." but if that doesn't feel quite right, you can use "I am becoming..." or "Every day I am getting more..."

♥ Ideas: I am a badass vixen babe. I am becoming the woman of my dreams. I am creative and delicious. I am a juicy peach! Every day, I am getting stronger. I am learning how to choose my thoughts. I am creating my reality every day. I am unstoppable. I AM THAT BITCH!

♥ Language is personal so use what works for you. It's okay to curse if it feels like that gives your affirmation extra KA-POW!

♥ Say your tapfirmation over and over in the mirror, looking yourself in the eye, tapping the points, until you feel the power really grow inside you. Then go out and conquer the world! Yes honey!

DON'T OBSERVE; CREATE

One of the reasons why we feel out of control of our own lives is because we are behaving as if we are simply passengers. Life appears to just "happen" to us, we feel victimized, and we continue to operate from that place. We fail to realize that we are the captains of our own ship, and we can point that bad boy anywhere we like.

Remember that this is your movie. You are the starlet, not a member of the audience! You are not just sitting around passively, munching popcorn, waiting for it to get good. No! You have the ability to spin any kind of world you want!

Existence feels so much better (and that's the point, right? To feel better!) when we become active participants in our own lives, when we stop looking at the conditions and reacting to them, and instead choose to CREATE the kind of life we want to have.

Releasing and allowing doesn't just mean sitting on your meditation cushion and watching the world go by. It means not suffering, not clinging to our hopes and wishes, and *fully* engaging with life! Finding joy, wherever that might be!

The joy might be in pottery classes, or it might be in hiking around Peru. It might be in going on a sailboat, or it might be in becoming a badass makeup artist. And it might be in all of these things!

Just because there is something you want and you don't have it right now, that is no excuse for the rest of your life to become sad and drab. The Universe responds to your *energy*, your frequency, your vibration, so your job is to do whatever it takes to bring the color back to your world!

This might mean quitting your job in favor of traveling the world, leaving your partner, or telling your parents you no longer want to be part of the family business. It is not always easy to do things like this, and may not feel like the path of least resistance. Perhaps in the moment it isn't, but when you look at it over a greater timeline, you'll see that it is.

It's easier to make a tough choice now than to suffer over three decades. And the process of cleaning up old habits, patterns and behaviors can sometimes look like it's getting messier before it gets better. But as the old saying goes, you have to crack some eggs if you want to make an omelette... And it's better to do it now, say no, break the cycle, than get dragged along by your hair for all eternity.

The most important thing is that you feel good about your life. The sooner you feel good, the faster things will flow to you. And here's a beautiful plot twist: as the rest of your life shores up and feels better, the less you will care about those things you "need" or were once obsessed over. And that speeds up their manifesting into reality even faster!

Babe, get out ahead of yourself and remember that *this is your life*. Make feeling good a priority and behave as if that is the only thing that matters. When you no longer have any tolerance for misery in your life, you will start making completely different decisions! The way you use your energy and the places you put your attention will change. Things will become clear. And you will be one of the people in the world who is truly in charge of their life.

This is something no one can ever take from you.

MOOD SWINGS AND BOUNCING BACK

Mood swings are a part of life. As often as you will be in the vortex, flying high and feeling ecstatic, there are going to be moments—many of them!—where you come crashing back down. Sometimes you'll be triggered by other people, and sometimes you'll be triggered by choosing miserable thoughts.

The most important thing to know about is that it's okay for this to happen. Don't beat yourself up for falling out of the vortex! In the beginning, that might be hard to do: you might feel really bad for losing your grip on those feelings. Again, it's okay! Don't feel bad for hopping out of the vortex and don't feel bad for feeling bad about it!

All that matters is that you get back to the vortex eventually, and you will. The more you practice this, the more evidence you will have that it's possible to get back there, and that it's easy to do so. Stay the course and keep the faith!

Truly magnificent manifesters are the ones who fall out of the vortex, notice it quickly, shrug it off, and go back there without too much hesitation. This is a muscle that you will build over time. Again, don't feel bad about it. You will get there!

(Remember, any time you fall out of the vortex is a gift. It provides you with a sense of contrast that helps you figure out what you want: go back and reread Chapter Three!)

KNOW WHAT YOU WANT, THEN LET IT GO

Trust me, I know: this can sound like an exercise in futility. It seems like a paradox in terms: if there's something swirling around in your head that you want desperately, more than anything else, how can you then not want it? How do you "let go" of something that occupies your mind, every waking moment?

The answer is that letting it go is a practice. A daily practice. An hourly practice. A practice that we must engage in minute-by-minute.

Because one of the most amazing things I've discovered, as I really dive deep into this work, is that when you are truly in the present moment, you don't want anything else.

Think back to the last time you were high on a moment. Maybe you were dancing in your living room; belting out a song at karaoke; walking the streets of New York in summer; swirling your tongue around a chocolate-dipped ice-cream cone. In that moment, as you were in full surrender to it, all of your senses alive and tingling, ecstatic in the vibrancy of that instant... Did you wish for anything else? Did you want anything to change? Did you hope for this or that?

The answer, of course, is no. In that moment, wherever you were, you were FULLY THERE. Totally engaged. Completely committed to whatever was going on. And that is where the real juice of life is. In those moments that completely engulf and envelop you.

So if there is something that you want more than anything, and you want to manifest it, and you don't know the next step? The only thing to do is get high on life.

There is no fiddling, no tampering, no jamming your fingers in pies. In fact, the more involved you become, the more you "try," the more effort you exert, the more you will make a muddle of things.

Let's say you are in love with someone. Your vision for what it could be is truly glorious: it's a big glowing neon sign, lit up with million megawatt bulbs. It's a hot pink sunset streaked through with orange and purple. My point is: the vision is beautiful. You know where you are going with them and what it looks like. But in the moments where you are just hanging out, laughing, are you fixated on the fact that you have not quite reached this destination yet? No! You are cracking up, looking into their eyes, seeing the love and joy within them, and deeply enjoying the moment.

Every single step of your journey with them is divine and beautiful and special and wonderful. And you are IN IT with them, absolutely relishing it, and ideally, not worrying about anything. You don't need to ask them to define it, because you can feel what it means based on their actions and their energy and how they treat you. You can see what it means when you look into their eyes. You don't need to ask them where it's going because as long as you continue feeling good and having fun, you know exactly where it's going: it's going in the direction of more of that.

There is no rush. Just enjoy where you are right now. It is delicious in this very instant. Suck all of the juice out of this very moment and let it fill your mouth.

You cannot have a happy ending to an unhappy journey. So be in the joy of it, every day, as much as you can.

This is what I mean by "Know what you want, and then let it go." Have your vision, and let it be glorious. And then stop trying to control everything, trying to wrap a periscope around the corner so you know what's ahead. What is ahead is what you're focusing on. What is ahead is what you keep thinking about. This mental and emotional discipline is *everything* and the importance of it cannot be overstated!

One of the things that has taken me a while to get my head around is that the Universe is always providing. I have a Post-It Note above my kitchen sink which says, "Miracles constantly arrive. My needs are always met." Some days, I need the reminder!

And when I can step into this belief and fully embody it, without restrictions or conditions—there is no "Well, the Universe provides for me when it comes to this subject but for THAT subject I need to get involved!" because this is a LAW and it works every time—then I am filled with relief. Calm descends over me. I lighten up and laugh again. I step back into the natural flow of life, and all of those things I was so worried about begin to resolve themselves, without me even having to lift a finger. It's quite amazing the way that it works.

That's what I love about the Law of Attraction. It always works, and the evidence is so clear and omnipresent.

I have to zoom out sometimes and remind myself that life is always happening for me, and not to me. I am not a victim of circumstance, and in fact, when things happen that may not feel good in the moment, I am always pleased when I look back at them, because they have helped to shape my world in such a positive way.

Everything is always working out for your highest good. Trust that.

KNOW WHAT YOU WANT, AND SAY NO TO THE REST

One of the ways that we can get really clear about what it is that we want, prove to the Universe that we are serious, and also make space in our lives to call in what we want, is to practice radical honesty. (This also means stepping away from people-pleasing, which is actually a form of covert manipulation. Dang!)

Here's an example from my past life, when I was actively dating. One of the ways that I would make things clear for the Universe was when I would go on a date and it wasn't a match, I would almost immediately let the man know this. Kindly, of course.

Let me explain.

I love people and I don't like hurting anyone. In the very olden days, if I went out with someone and I didn't want to see them again, I would just drift away. I didn't want to make someone feel bad by telling them I didn't like them! What a nightmare. Yes, it's true: I would ghost them. Slowly! Ugh, terrible!

I used to think that the best way not to hurt someone was to be indirect, but now I have changed my tune.

It's much healthier—and in higher integrity—to grit your teeth and send a text message which goes something like, "Hey ____! Thanks so much for last night, I had a good time and you're really awesome. I've been thinking about it and I think we would be better off as friends."

You will probably not enjoy doing this, but you are being "cruel" in order to be kind. And while the act won't bring you joy, it does in fact feel good, because you are acting in integrity. You are keeping your energetic side of the street clean. You don't want to lead anyone on—that only creates more problems—and every time we make it clear to the Universe what we want and *do not want*, it can deliver our dreams with even more speed and precision.

HOW TO FEEL BETTER ABOUT MANIFESTING

When you start to dabble with the Law of Attraction—or hell, even years into the practice—you may suffer from moments of doubt, skepticism, even downright disbelief.

'Yes, I know all of this manifesting stuff,' you may find yourself thinking. 'And I'm doing it all the right way! So what am I doing wrong?! Where IS the love of my love? Why is the money not in my bank account? Where is the evidence of my manifesting abilities?'

The problem is in the question itself. We get so hung up on the physical manifestations and think that they are the only way to know whether this stuff is "working" or not.

Don't use your observational senses to take score of how far along you are in the process of manifesting, because often, the things we desire manifest in the blink of an eye! It's true, isn't it? So your eyes and ears are actually not a reliable measuring stick. The babe of your dreams could be right around the corner and you'd never know it.

You should only use how you feel as a way of measuring how close you are.

The only time that something is slow to manifest—because it is always coming to you—is when you are trying too hard. Giving it too much of the wrong kind of attention. Thinking about it more and more. Nothing will change this way.

Think about why you want it, the emotional reason for it, a way that makes you feel good. Find a way to think about it that feels better.

What is the why behind what you want?

The truth is that you don't really want the thing. You want the feeling you think the thing will give you.

But once you realize you can have that feeling *right now*, by sinking into the moment and seeking out fun, you will be less attached to needing this specific thing. When you truly practice this, you can cut out the middle man—i.e., that thing you think you need—and just sink into the delight of enjoying your life at this moment!

Some people will chase that carrot their entire lives, always hunting down the next thing they think will give them the feeling they crave. If you remain oblivious to the fact that you can generate that feeling, right now, with no external factors, you will always be in pain. You will always look outside of yourself for happiness.

We all have hopes and dreams. Sometimes they can seem overwhelming, and we can get totally freaked out if we start to think that maybe it's not going to turn out the way we want it to. But the truth is that none of us are guaranteed tomorrow. In fact, there is no security in life, period.

Let's take romance as an example. Even if you meet someone amazing, even if you got together, even if you got engaged, even if you got married, even if you had babies and bought a house, that doesn't guarantee another instant of happiness. It doesn't create any real sense of security, because who's to say that one of you won't get hit by a truck tomorrow? When we put all this pressure on the future, or when we see the future as a place where we will one day eventually "arrive," we are fooling ourselves. All that we truly have is NOW. My advice is to make the most of it!

TRAIN YOURSELF TO LOOK AT WHAT YOU LIKE

Learning to focus on things that please you rather than things that upset you is a *skill* and a discipline!

Think about the last time you had a blemish on your face. I am willing to bet you money that every time you looked in the mirror, that's exactly where your eye went! In fact, maybe you even took a kind of sick pleasure in honing in on your flaw and being upset about it. You just kept looking at that pimple, wishing it was different, wishing you weren't so hideous today... Instead of looking at your beautiful eyes, or how luscious your hair is looking, or any number of other things!

Next time you have a blemish, practice looking at something else when you're in front of the mirror. This is a way of retraining your brain not to obsess over scarcity, lack, and the things you don't enjoy. Humans have a negativity bias that is built-in as part of our evolution, but you can change your brain by *doing different things!*

Don't go hunting out things that you know will upset you! Why bother? Just leave it alone! Don't fill your brain with all that mess. Keep your channel clear, honey.

DON'T BE PATIENT, BE CONFIDENT

"Those who are certain of the outcome can afford to wait, and wait without anxiety." —A Course in Miracles

The goal with manifesting is to feel so good about it, and so sure about it, that you don't need to be "patient." You can just be certain and calm.

Imagine, if you will, someone who is confident that what they want is coming. They do not run around in a flap, freaking out, nervous and nutty. No! They get dressed up to greet the day and they *enjoy their life.*

Don't put everything on hold while you wait for things to come to fruition. Nothing will slow the process down more effectively! Know what you want, bless it, and *let it go* while you enjoy the rest of your life.

Your energy is a precious resource and the way that you use it is infinitely important! Pour all that energy—the energy that you were using to nervously fret about the thing you want—into creating a beautiful world for yourself. Dream it up, envision the life you'd like to live, and then start concocting it!

THE KEY TO MANIFESTING IS TO LET THE PRESENT FEEL OVERWHELMINGLY GOOD

"To be happy with yourself in the present moment while maintaining a dream of your future is a grand recipe for manifestation. When you feel so whole that you no longer care whether 'it' will happen, that's when amazing things materialize before your eyes. I've learned that being whole is the perfect state of creation. I've seen this time and time again in witnessing true healings in people all over the world. They feel so complete that they no longer want, no longer feel lack, and no longer try to do it themselves. They let go, and to their amazement, something greater than they are responds—and they laugh at the simplicity of the process." —Dr. Joe Dispenza

I'm obsessed with this quote, and my favorite part is *being whole is the perfect state of creation.*

It's absolutely true. The easiest way to let go of our attachment to what we want, to stop future-tripping, and to chill out in general, is to enjoy the moment as much as possible. There is really no other way.

Cast your mind back to the last time that you finally let go of a desire, and how good that felt! When you do this, your entire being relaxes and expands. It's like your higher self finally let their shoulders drop, and a feeling of calmness washes over you.

Grasping never gets us what we want. In fact, the more we grasp, the more it slips away from us, like sand through our fingers! The thing about grasping is that we're doing it because we believe that this thing we want is our only salvation... But you already know, by now, that no one thing is your salvation. Nothing outside of you will really give you the feeling that you want! Only you can do that.

Think about that. Take a deep breath. Breathe in the knowledge that you already have everything you need within you, and let it inflate you and fill you up. Then visualize yourself blowing the desire and attachment out of your body.

This is how we unblock our blessings: by not needing anything external. By relaxing. By settling deeply into the moment like it's a fluffy bubble bath.

And then... Just like magic... When you finally let it go, everything comes rushing in. You have released the desire and you have allowed the Universe to do its work. What a beautiful thing. ✳

STEP 3: RELEASE AND ALLOW

06

LIVE YOUR FANTASY

N THE WORLD OF THE LAW OF ATTRACTION, PEOPLE BANDY around a lot of terms that feel a bit old hat. One of these phrases is "living as if," the idea being that you need to live as *if* the thing you want is already here. But that phrase, "living as if," lacks a certain... Je ne sais quoi. I prefer to LIVE YOUR FANTASY!

What does it mean to live your fantasy?

It means that you *go all out*, honey! It means that you surround yourself with the people, things, and experiences that you really love. It means that you do whatever it takes to bring the things you want into your life. It means that you live it up!

But before you ask, here's what it *doesn't* mean! It doesn't mean getting yourself into debt because you are spending beyond what you can handle. No ma'am. Believe me when I say that you don't need to spend extravagantly to bring your fantasy to fruition! And it also doesn't mean that you lie to others about your accomplishments, skills or knowledge. Honesty and integrity is everything.

Living your fantasy means getting yourself into energetic alignment with the things that you want. If you want to be in a relationship, act like you are in one! (Buy yourself a cute engagement ring and wear it around the house!) If you want a hot new car, act like the kind of person who would drive that car. It is important to *close the energetic gap* between where you are now, and where you would like to be.

Ask yourself, "If I were the kind of person who had X, how would I behave?"

You will be amazed by what floats into your consciousness by simply asking yourself this question. It is one of the quickest and easiest ways to sync up your behavior with the person you would like to be. You will find yourself picking up your energetic socks, if you will.

Let's say, for example, that you want to have a business that turns over seven figures. This is not impossible, not by a long shot. But it probably requires you to behave differently, and to run your life in a new and improved way.

Maybe the version of you who runs a seven figure business does not flake on social engagements. She is diligent about outsourcing the things she is not good at, and only does things within her zone of genius. She is probably well-organized and tidy. She doesn't date anyone who is threatened by her success... And she doesn't work in her pajamas!

Then again, maybe she does! Maybe she swans around in a marabou robe until 2pm! Only you know the answer!

How about we use relationships as another example? If what you really want is to be in a fulfilling, beautiful relationship, how would that version of you behave? Well, maybe she wouldn't go to the bar several nights a week. Maybe she wouldn't have female friends who distrust men. Maybe she would keep her bedroom looking luscious, more like a goddess sex temple than a scrap-heap! Again: who knows?! It's up to you!

Write down a list of all the things that you are currently manifesting (as if you have already manifested them, if you please). Go through them one-by-one and ask yourself, "If I were the kind of person who had this, was doing this, had obtained this, how would I behave?" Make notes of everything that comes up. You may be surprised by what your subconscious spits out. This is a wonderful exercise to uncover what you really believe about success, and what it looks like for you.

The truth is that only you hold the energetic keys to whatever you are creating. If you believe that you need to be organized in order to run a seven figure business, *you will not have a seven figure business until you get organized.*

Once you are aware of the beliefs you have around obtaining these things, you have three choices. You can raise your standards and begin to behave as your idealized self—which is pretty sexy!—or you can use tapping to dismantle the beliefs. The third option is that you can do both! This is what I recommend.

Why not raise your standards so that you feel good about yourself, while *simultaneously* removing the energetic hooks? Because this criteria that you are holding onto, well-meaning and helpful though it may be, is actually a limiting belief!

Raising your expectations of how you behave is such a powerful thing to do. Creating new standards for yourself, and then living up to them, will help you build self-esteem. If you decide to change something, you follow through and then remain committed to that change, you will feel so good about yourself. As your standards change, your behavior will too, and so will everything else. The people around you will either grow to meet you or fall away. The experiences you have will start to shift. Your tolerance for other people's poor behavior, and even your own moods, will transform too. This will help you manifest more quickly and powerfully than ever before.

If you couple raising your standards with tapping on your limiting beliefs, your growth will be stratospheric.

HOUSE-WITCHERY ON FLEEK

You contain an immense amount of power within your body and spirit. As we move through this book, you have been uncovering the enormous number of ways in which your life can change by simply changing your thoughts or using your body differently.

But your physical self isn't the only conductor of energy. Your home conducts energy too.

You can look at somebody's home and tell what is going on with them at a metaphysical level. Is their home messy, dirty, disorganized? Is it neglected? Are they hoarding? Does everything in their home work (doorknobs, windows, curtains)... Or is it full of broken appliances, dead light bulbs, and abandoned projects?

Have you ever walked past a house that has grass and weeds growing a foot high in the garden, with a front door hanging off its hinges and broken shutters? Tell me: when you walk past a home like that, do you ever think that something really wonderful is going on inside it?!

I have yet to meet a happy, successful, thriving person whose home was in complete disarray.

Please note: complete disarray is not the same thing as a creative mess! I, like many of you, leave a little tornado behind me as I move through my day, thinking up a million ideas and getting distracted. But—and it's a big but!—I also tidy up after myself! I get broken things fixed (and often do it myself). I take exquisite care of my home. It is my sanctuary, and my creative temple, and as such, I like it to be in tip-top order.

There are many facets to living well, and along with making feeling good your priority and questioning your thoughts, tending to your home is right up there.

Our homes are an extension of us, and so the way that you treat your home is a reflection of how you feel about yourself. Do you look after yourself, or do you treat yourself as if you are an afterthought? Do you go to the doctor, the dentist, the gym? Do you have systems in your life that make daily living easier? I promise that you can see the answers to those questions in your home!

It is impossible to feel good in a disaster zone.

House-witchery covers the multitude of ways in which we can infuse our homes with magic. From feng shui to color psychology to traditional witchcraft, there are so many things we can do to raise the energy levels of our homes... And in turn, ourselves.

HAVING AN ABUNDANT HOME

When people come to my house, they often say, "I don't feel comfortable in many people's homes, but I always feel good in your space."

To me, this is the ultimate compliment. It's very important to me to create a space that is warm, welcoming, comfortable, fun and practical, and what could be better than creating an environment that makes your friends and lovers feel good?

So, what can you do to foster these feelings within your own space?

First of all, you have to keep it clean. This is truly non-negotiable. Nothing is more low vibration than a dirty, messy, disorganized home. Lord have mercy.

If you don't love cleaning and tidying, do what you have to do to fit it into your life somehow. If you make cleaning a time when you get to listen to your favorite podcasts, do that! If you need to watch those shows about cleaning and organizing to glean inspiration, do that! If you have the budget to hire a housekeeper, have one come by, even if it's only once a month!

I do not, personally, relish cleaning, but I do my best. I have a robot vacuum cleaner which runs every day, and then I have a housekeeper come every week. She cleans my house from top to bottom and leaves it looking perfect. I do my dishes every night, I put my shoes away when I get home, and I put things back in their place once I use them.

Trust me, I was not always this tidy... But years of living with messy men flipped a switch! These days, I absolutely love having an immaculate house, and I strive to keep it that way.

Having a well-stocked home is also very abundant. This doesn't need to cost a lot of money, but it does require being organized. Why would you buy one roll of toilet paper at a time when you could buy a jumbo pack?

I like to keep my kitchen filled with favorite snacks, too. A cursory glance inside the refrigerator will turn up enough delights to thrill any guest. There's kombucha, gluten-free ice-cream cones, tuna salad, vegan chocolates, garlic dip, and enough oat milk to keep me in frothy lattes until kingdom come. In my pantry, you'll find endless amounts of coffee, supplements, and tortilla chips.

Even though I did a massive clear-out when I moved from New York to California, I kept the things that were truly essential. My home in California is well-curated but also extremely well-stocked. I am seldom stumped by anything a guest might need! I am like a Girl Scout, truly equipped for every necessity. Need a Band-Aid? False eyelashes? A floral turban? Medicine? A hot water bottle? I have all those things—and I know exactly where they are, too.

Having a home that makes sense is such a simple thing to do, all it requires is a little bit of organization. And beyond it making your life easier—which it certainly does—a very compelling reason to do this is that it keeps you feeling abundant.

We get more of what we believe, and we believe what we experience, so if your experience is that there is *always more than enough*, it keeps that little sense of desperation, lack, or scarcity from creeping in. Definitely a good practice.

SEEDING THE ENERGY IN YOUR HOME

When you move into a house, it is just a space: four walls and a door. It doesn't have any meaning. It is simply a piece of construction. Just like our own lives, the meaning our homes have is the meaning we *bring*. It is for this reason that it is essential to seed your energy in your home.

What I mean by this is that we plant ourselves, energetically, in our houses. We sow seeds, metaphorically, and allow them to grow.

Everything you bring into your home is telling a story. When you are purchasing furniture, are you buying it desperately, snapping up whatever is on sale, even if it isn't perfect? Or do you take your time, wait for the right item, and save up for the things you love?

The art on your walls—or lack thereof—tells a story too. My office in my current home is like a living vision board, with art covering every single wall. It is massively inspiring to me! There are iconic prints from Slim Aarons, paintings of women I love, framed photographs from my birthday, portraits other people have painted of me, neon signs, and so much more. There's something delightful no matter where your eye lands, and I love it.

Do you have photos up in your home, and if so, how do they make you feel? If you have a falling out with someone, or if seeing their picture brings back unpleasant memories, take down those images! When one of my ex-boyfriends and I broke up, I took down all the photos of us immediately. I wanted to close that chapter of my life, and I did!

Ask yourself, 'What am I seeding in this space? How are my thoughts and actions influencing what happens in my home? Who am I opening my door to, and what are they bringing into my life?'

The people in your life dictate the quality of your life. When you meet someone new, ask yourself, 'Would I want this person in my home?' If you wouldn't want to invite them inside, take that to heart! If you wouldn't want them in your living room, for God's sake, don't sleep with them!

Your home is a sacred space and it should be treated as such. Be mindful about the words you speak inside your home, the company you keep, and the art you hang on the walls. If it helps you to think of it as a temple, then do so! You don't need your home to be like everyone else's. Create a space that works for you, that sustains your positive feelings, that inspires and uplifts you.

MODERN SPACE-CLEARING FOR MYSTICS

Space-clearing is simply the act of circulating energy and not allowing it to grow stagnant.

There are an infinite number of ways that we can clear the energy in our homes. Usually when we think about this, we grab a bundle of sage or maybe a stick of palo santo. We light up a stick of incense and wave it around. But the coolest thing about magic is that there are no hard and fast rules about any of this. In fact, the only essential thing that is required in magic is intention!

Here are a few of my favorite—perhaps unconventional—ways to clear your space and get the energy moving.

♥ SOUND

Music is magic, and one of the things I do every single day, without fail, is to flood my home with music that I love. I have speakers in every room (an absolutely worthwhile investment), and I *crank* my favorite songs.

Sound is vibration, and playing different sounds shakes up the energy of a space. Think about the effect that your favorite songs have on your mood—why would your home be any different?

If you've ever had a sound bath, you know how deeply sound can impact us, unlock parts of us, and elevate us. Playing music is like giving your whole house a sound bath! So whether you love to dance around to the latest pop, the best of Bad Boy Records, or you prefer the tones of Tibetan singing bowls, TURN IT UP!

The morning is an especially potent time to play magical tones. If you have favorite mantras, binaural beats, or even affirmation tracks, the morning is such a delicious time to play them. I love a Lakshmi chant first thing—what a vibe!

Let the walls of your bedroom soak up thumping beats or calming mantras. Bring a hot new energy to your home office. Turn your living room into a pop temple, complete with dance moves. Allow the magic of music to transform your space.

♥ LIGHT

I admit it: I am a light junkie. I cannot get enough. One of the reasons why I love the home I'm in is because it is absolutely flooded with light all day long. So, why not go all out? My home is full of items to catch the light and disperse it... And it feels so good! I have solar-powered rainbow-makers in my windows, mirror balls balanced on top of light fixtures, and crystals dangling in front of sunbeams.

As the sun shifts through my house, some new item is illuminated and sends a shower of light across my space. Mirror balls explode outwards like flowers in bloom, rainbow-makers sweep around in a circular motion like a psychic broom, and crystals radiate a kaleidoscope of color onto the wall.

Yes, these things look incredible, and yes, it is like living in an ever-evolving theater where—depending on the time of the day—different magic tricks are being performed. But there is also a metaphysical element at play.

This light performs a clearing, cleaning my home and keeping the energy in motion. We are irrefutably affected by light. Harnessing the natural light that circulates throughout my home shifts the vibe, brightens dark corners, and reminds me of the inherent magic of the universe. Best of all, it costs almost nothing to do.

♥ AIR

Living in California is a totally different experience than being on the East Coast. People here really bring the outdoors in, and the environment is woven into their homes seamlessly. Every morning here, as I make my coffee, I walk to the big sliding door that accesses my balcony and open it up. I let the ocean breeze blow in and cleanse my home. It feels sublime.

I know this is such a simple idea—to crack a window!—but it is a powerful one, and it's one I like being reminded of. Growing up, the house we lived in didn't have a lot of windows that could be opened, and then once I moved to New York, I wouldn't open the windows very often because it was either a) too loud, b) too hot, c) too cold, or d) too dirty, and I didn't want car exhaust floating in and leaving soot on my windowsill.

These days, I am extremely blessed to be living in a place that is quiet, with lovely temperatures and a beautiful view. So if you're in an environment that permits you to, I want to encourage you to open your windows in the morning, even if it is only for a few minutes.

Open your windows to greet the day, and let fresh energy into your home. And if it is safe for you to do so, sleep with your windows open too. I always experience more restful sleep when there is fresh air circulating in my bedroom, and my dreams are more lush too.

♥ SCENT

Have you ever walked into a beautiful boutique or an extravagant hotel and noticed how good it smells? I have, and it's one of my favorite types of experiences. I love the attention to detail, and I love how individual it is. Every space smells different, and it is completely tailored to the kind of experience they want to give you.

It probably makes sense, then, that I am a nut for scent. I adore scented candles and essential oils, and always have one or the other going.

It's important that you are making healthy choices for your home. I wouldn't personally recommend those scented plug-in devices, simply because they are loaded with chemicals. Instead, I suggest buying good quality essential oils or candles made by small businesses.

When it comes to essential oils, I put a few drops in a diffuser and let it simmer. I love to use lavender essential oil in my bedroom, eucalyptus in the bathroom, and sweet orange in the kitchen!

Another thing you can do is use a chunk of a bubble bar from Lush instead of regular detergent. Just throw it in the washing machine! It will get your clothes just as clean—I promise!—but they will come out smelling delicious. This is a great trick for washing blankets or even dog beds!

HOT FENG SHUI FIXES

Feng shui is an ancient art with oodles of modern-day application. You can go really deep into it, or you can just skim the surface and still get loads of value. Here are a few feng shui fixes that you can apply to your home right now!

❤ DOTE ON YOUR FRONT DOOR

Your front door should be clean and the numbers on it (or next to it) should be clear and legible! If you have lights at your front door or around the property, they should all be functioning. Why is this? Your front door is where energy enters, and it is how opportunity finds you! How can opportunity knock—literally—if it's unsure which house you live in?! Clean your front door regularly, and then wipe it down with citrus essential oils to attract prosperity!

❤ STOKE THE SOULMATE VIBES

Want to attract more love into your life? Put paired items in your bedroom! If you can splurge on matching bedside tables and matching lamps, go for it. A pair of rose quartz crystal towers is a lovely addition too! If you've been single for longer than you'd like, get rid of any artwork featuring a solitary figure, and either hang art that features a couple, or something that shows an open landscape.

❤ UP YOUR ABUNDANCE

First things first: don't ever put your handbag or wallet on the floor! (Respect the bag, baby!) Always have fresh flowers in your home: they symbolize abundance, and the water in the vase helps draw in money too. Don't hoard things; this is like shouting at the Universe that you're afraid of not having enough. And a tip from me? Buy yourself a Cash Cannon, fill it with a stack of fake $100 bills, squeeze the trigger, and throw yourself a prosperity party every week!

❤ MOVE 27 THINGS
Any time you feel like the vibe in your home is low, make a practice of moving 27 items. Rearrange a drawer, swap the cushions, move your photographs, drag your plants to the opposite corner... It doesn't matter as long as you move 27 things!

❤ PASS THE SALT
Salt is big in all mystical traditions. One of my favorite ways to use it is to sprinkle a line of it across my threshold—just behind my front door—to protect my space. This tactic works miracles. Last time I did this was because I was intent on creating an energetic barrier between myself and someone else, and let me tell you: they never darkened my door again.

❤ SCRAP THE SENTIMENT
If you have recently been through a break-up or divorce, consider the items that you are still holding onto and what kind of energy they might contain. When my ex-husband and I got divorced, he took our old mattress with him when he moved out, and I bought a new one. Then, before I moved to Los Angeles, my best friend and I dragged that mattress down onto the street. Begone! Also be sure to ask yourself whether you want to keep the gifts that old lovers have given you. What is the value in holding onto them? I gave my engagement ring back to my ex-husband, and sold the jewelry one of my ex-boyfriends had bought me. I didn't need those things in my orbit anymore.

❤ CLEAR THE CLUTTER
As my friend Amanda Gibby Peters says, "Clutter is an energy vampire." We don't even notice how much its presence is sucking joy from us until we finally get around to clearing it up! Even those little clutter moments—small stacks of books on the floor, the pile of unread mail in the kitchen, the jumble of laundry—are stealing effervescence from your life! See if you can make a practice of clearing up one small area of clutter every day.

KEEP YOUR CHANNEL CLEAR

If you're feeling drained or pessimistic, it's important to get curious about what you are *feeding yourself*. By this, I don't just mean food! I also encourage you to take a close look at what you're watching, reading, and scrolling through.

By now, we all know that social media can be damaging to our mental health, which of course impacts how we are feeling. It's essential that we are proactive in unfollowing accounts that make us feel less than wonderful! It's also immensely helpful to set social media limits, or even delete apps when we're not using them.

But that's not all. We also need to think about the movies, TV shows and YouTube channels we watch, and the music, podcasts, and audiobooks we listen to.

I am absolutely fastidious about what I consume because it all comes out in my mood, and therefore my work. As someone who is deeply entrenched in the self-development space, and as someone who sees a responsibility to live as an example, I cannot dabble with anything that doesn't make me feel good. This rule is hard and fast, and it applies to everything from what I eat, to who I get into a relationship with, to the movies I watch.

When it comes to movies and television, I really only watch comedy, documentaries and reality television that either provides inspiration or escapism. As much as I was fascinated by serial killers as a teenager, I am not drawn to watch, say, the latest greatest murder documentary. That kind of thing doesn't fuel me and definitely won't provide me with anything useful I can utilize later.

The content you consume has a cumulative effect on how you feel and how you view the world. Here in the western world, we have been groomed since birth to become less and less sensitive to the insanity on television, so this is an insidious issue. There is no absolute right or wrong, but being aware of what we are feeding our brains with could never be a bad thing.

WHAT ARE YOU WEARING?

Everything in your life is telling a story and deepening a belief that you have, even the way that you adorn yourself. If you are on the Feeling Good Train (choo choo!), there is absolutely no way that you should be wearing anything that does not move you closer to your desires, doesn't speak volumes about who you want to be, and doesn't allow you to move through the world in a way that reinforces your worthiness.

If your fantasy is to buy a hot black Porsche, then you should be dressing in a way that makes you feel like you could walk into the dealership today and feel absolutely confident about that.

One of the best things I learned from taking striptease dance classes is that the world believes what you believe. That is to say, if you feel sexy and believe that you are sexy, whoever is looking at you will buy into that story. I remember taking a private class with my friend Jillian, and I was practicing my body waves. I was overthinking it a lot. She said to me, "Don't think about how to do it. You KNOW how to do it. Just DO it. Be the person who KNOWS how to do it."

Guess what? As soon as I applied that mindset, I nailed those body waves. They were effortless!

This is a lesson that can be applied to every single thing in your life. Think about the last time you had great sex. Not just sex that was alright, but sex that blew your mind. When I do this, I am reminded of a recent time when the sex was so good that the next morning, there was make-up smudged on the wall. (Both foundation and eyeliner. Top marks!)

Your latest and greatest sexcapades may not have done permanent damage to your soft furnishings, but no matter! Ruminate on what that sexual experience was like. Ask yourself, in those moments, was your partner looking at you nervously, constantly checking that they were doing an okay job? Or were they *owning* themselves, giving you a look like they were about to devour you, and acting confidently and decisively?

In my example, my partner took me like he had been thinking about it *all day long*. (Later investigation turned out that, yes, this was indeed the case!) He performed as if he knew he could make me feel good. And it was infinitely hot.

This is really the secret between the people who "have it" and the people who don't. The people who truly HAVE IT just ACT like they have it!

I remember being in my friend's backyard a few years ago, hanging out with none other than Carmen Electra. It was our first time meeting, and she was so sweet, and extremely normal! We were chit-chatting on the grass, watching as a huge rig was being erected over the swimming pool. It had a hook in the middle that you could attach yourself to using elaborate rope-work. Carmen wanted to play with it, because she is a dancer, and as soon as she was attached to the rig, she completely transformed. She went from being a lovely woman on the grass to a full-blown performer. In a black bodysuit, fishnets, and Dr Marten boots, she was endlessly elegant, making shapes over the water, moving effortlessly and gracefully as we all watched on, awe-struck.

Being nervous in front of a camera or a crowd never works. It doesn't translate. You can see, smell, and feel the fear. People who are afraid of being seen have no presence. You already know this to be true. So *why* would it be any different in real life? People who are afraid of LIFE have no presence either!

Don't worry: it's easily solved. If you are afraid of life, the best antidote is to act as if you are not. If you want something, the best thing to do is act as if you already have it. We need to be constantly strutting that line between our current situation and where we want to be.

Our appearance is a public service announcement. With it, you can let people know that you are to be respected... Or that you don't think much of yourself. And the way that we broadcast will have an instant impact on the kind of response we receive.

We would be insane to think that we exist in a vacuum and that the way we dress, hold ourselves, and look at other people will not garner a reaction. You have a reaction to every single person you see, so why would the rules not apply to you?

In many ways, knowing this is a gift. Once you become fully aware of this fact, then you are free to decide *how* you would like people to see you. Would you like them to be inspired by you, or would you prefer to move through the world unseen? Do you want people to lust after you, would you like to be worshiped and revered? Do you want to appear powerful... Or mythical? Or something else?

Instagram can be such a potent place. I'll never forget seeing a photo of a tattoo which said, "Sad sexy woman." My face just fell. I can't judge her for doing it, because I was once in that exact place—where my sadness felt like an integral part of my personality—but I do remember how bad it felt. And when we take these beliefs about ourselves and tattoo them on our bodies, or even wear a T-shirt that says, "Boys lie" or "Cruel World", how can we expect to evolve, move forward, and choose better thoughts?

Don't get me wrong, I love a graphic tee as much as anyone, but I am extremely deliberate about what I buy. I will never buy clothing that literally *says something about me* that I wouldn't say about myself, or wouldn't allow someone else to say about me! No thank you. Instead, I like to wear chokers that say "Queen" in sparkly rhinestones! I get tattoos that say "Radical Self Love" and "High Vibe Honey"! Words are so powerful: which ones are you choosing to represent you?

I remember going to see Elton John perform at the Staples Center with my parents. I didn't have much time to prepare my outfit, but as soon as I thought about who we were going to see—the king of amazing eye-wear and extravagant looks—I knew I had to *bring it!* I ended up wearing a purple wig, gold rhinestone-encrusted glasses, a black bodysuit, silver sequin trousers, a purple leopard print faux-fur coat, and sparkly silver ankle boots. It was an INSANE outfit... And I had literally never felt better. All night long, I got the most incredible reactions, and it reminded me of the power of really dressing to express.

Colors amplify your aura. Consider the magic of tone and hue, and how it makes you feel when you wear it. There are a few hues that increase my personal power by several orders of magnitude: fuchsia, baby pink, lavender, and sky blue. I feel unbelievably good in these colors! I also feel really great in white or grey. By contrast, even though I think black looks sleek and chic, it doesn't get my motor running like a punchy palette does, so I wear less of it than I used to.

We would be foolish to think that we do not change a room by walking into it—everyone does. We all bring our own unique essence, and we all bring our own energy. The question is: what are you bringing? When you walk into a room and you feel good, you are vibrating high, you are in the vortex, *everyone notices it.* Everyone feels it. Most people will be buoyed by your presence, uplifted, inspired. Some people will not, but that is not your problem. Why not walk through this world bringing all you can, in every moment?

Let's TURN UP our fantasies! Why live a drab lifestyle when you could be living performance art?

There is an old saying: "Don't dress for the job that you have, dress for the job you want."

Let's expand that.

Don't dress for the life that you have, dress for the life that you want. This is exactly why I have closets overflowing with multicolored faux furs, crystal-covered high heels, psychedelic turbans, sequin dresses, jeweled kaftans from Morocco, and, well, basically everything you could think of. Do I wear pink crystal aviator sunglasses to a weekday lunch date? YES!

Live your fantasy!

Like everything, your mileage on this may vary. Your inspirations might be different than mine: less drag queen, and more Diane Keaton. We are all different! But whoever it is that lights you up, follow that impulse! Life is an experiment, a playground where you get to try out anything and everything that thrills you. Flirting with different parts of your personality through your appearance can be a deeply fulfilling and satisfying experience!

For more on this, see my first book, *Radical Self-Love: A Guide To Loving Yourself And Living Your Dreams.* And for a top secret insight into what your true aesthetic dreams really look like, do some research into your Venus sign!

THE SECRET TO LIVING YOUR FANTASY

The biggest secret to living your fantasy is to detach as much as possible from worrying about what people think about you. As long as you are concerned with the opinions of the masses, you will always hold yourself back, and never be able to fully express yourself.

Think about your favorite people: icons from history, revolutionaries, stars of the silver screen. While they were all human, and of course prone to regular human feelings, one of the things that truly catapulted them to success (and worldwide renown) is that they were able to squash the majority of their fears around *how other people felt* about what they were doing.

All of the people that I really look up to—the Salvador Dalis, the Madonnas, the Diana Vreelands—were so in love with their vision of *how it could be* that they simply didn't have time to listen to the peanut gallery. Can you imagine how anticlimactic Dali's career would have been if he had been deterred by the critics? Do you think Madonna would have ascended to the absolute top of the pop world if she really been afraid of the Vatican? Would Diana Vreeland have lived as fully if she had taken her firing from *Vogue* personally?

No matter how well you tend to your vibration, things will happen in your life that are outside of your control. People will surprise you; you will experience pain and loss; there will be twists and turns that you could never predict.

But it is your choice as to how much you allow these things to affect you. You can allow pain to close your heart, critics to shut your creativity, and the unforeseen to derail you... Or you can remain committed to LIVING YOUR FANTASY. You can use the pain to fuel you as you soar even higher. You can let the satisfaction of proving people wrong be an aphrodisiac as you make love to the universe, and manifest your dreams. ✳

"Be alone. Eat alone, take yourself on dates, sleep alone. In the midst of this you will learn about yourself. You will grow, you will figure out what inspires you, you will curate your own dreams, your own beliefs, your own stunning clarity, and when you do meet the person who makes your cells dance, you will be sure of it, because you are sure of yourself."—Bianca Sparacino

07

MANIFESTING THE LOVE OF YOUR LIFE

Y LOVE, PLEASE, PUT ON YOUR SEATBELT. BECAUSE I am about to take you to a place that you were not, perhaps, anticipating.

It is time for us to do some serious appraisal of whether the people we are in partnership with are *truly right for us*. Whether they are bringing the right kind of energy. Whether they are elevating or denigrating us. Whether we are squandering our time, effort, and energy on the people we choose to bring into our lives.

This is an announcement to my single babes *just as much* as my coupled-up cuties! No matter whether you have been single for a long time or married for ten years, you still need to ask yourself these questions.

One of the delicious perks of the work I do is the sheer amount of incredible women I get to meet at events, on the street, through social media, and the list goes on. The thing that is so shocking is the sheer number of them who do not truly see themselves. They are apologetic about who they are, they have not stepped into their own power, and they are living at about 20% of their true capacity.

Sound familiar, babycakes?

Here's something you need to know about yourself.

You are powerful. You glow. You are magnetic and full of delicious energy.

Because of this, and precisely because you are potent and precious, anyone who you allow into your life is *lucky*. They are blessed! They get to be around you, enjoy your energy and bask in your presence. They get to recharge off your vibe!

The question we need to be asking ourselves is *what are they bringing to the table?*

Truly.

You already contain *absolutely everything you will ever need*. Love is magical and wonderful, but it is so dangerous to think that we require another person in order to be complete. It is simply not true. I want you to recognize that.

Finding someone, starting to date, falling in love, even getting married: all of those things are easy. It happens every single day to millions of people. But what is also easy is getting into a relationship with someone who is not on your energetic wavelength, and allowing them to snuff out your light.

I can say this with absolute authority because this is something I have struggled with, on and off, my entire life. I down-dated so much I practically got my Masters in it. I have suffered from the illness of "wanting to be picked" without thinking, 'Wait, what is this person truly contributing to my life?'

I love to be in relationships, like most of us do! Creating a life with someone is a truly beautiful thing. But being in a relationship with the wrong person is absolutely brutal.

Now, this doesn't mean that we should be single for the rest of our lives, because what if it all goes wrong again. But so many of us get into relationships with people who are simply not right for us. People who bring us down, rather than people who uplift us.

You are a grown adult now, and so I want you to start thinking more deeply than *are they cute and do they like me?* If creating an exceptional life is something you desire—and I believe it is, or you wouldn't be here reading this!—then you truly need to appraise every potential suitor carefully.

As you move through your life, the criteria by which you assess them will change. It's very normal when you're young to be mostly obsessed with looks and height, but I daresay that as you grow and mature, the things that really matter to you will shift.

For example, before I met the man I'm with now, I was very clear that my next significant partner could not be someone who would be threatened by the pink Lamborghini parked in my garage! And while this may seem kind of hilarious and frivolous, it actually isn't. A partner who has anything but positive feelings about your ambition and/or success is a major red flag!

Merging your life with someone else's is one of the most significant things you can do, and that is because *their life becomes your life* (and vice versa). If it gets serious, you will probably end up living together, spending time with each others' friends, and participating in—or at least talking about—each others' interests. Your lives truly will merge. So when you are going on dates and getting to know someone, it is absolutely essential to ask yourself, 'What would our life together look like? And is this a life I want?'

In the last chapter, we discussed homes as a metaphor for what is going on with a person. So now, let's use that information and tie it to relationships.

I lived with a man who was a "collector", but it almost bordered on hoarding. His place was absolutely loaded to the gills with vintage stuff. He didn't like to clean, and he was so anal about his things that he wouldn't even let *me* move anything to clean around it. It was like living inside an asthma attack. It was so embarrassing that I would never invite friends over. What can we deduce about his character from his home? He was so rigid and allergic to change that when his industry shifted, he simply couldn't move with it. He left his job and would not get another one. By the time we broke up, he was so down on his luck that he had been priced out of New York City and had to move to another state.

Another time, I dated a man whose house was so gross that I hated being there. I refused to walk around it without socks on. There were sheets stapled to the window instead of curtains, the lightbulbs were always blown out, and there was a hole in the wall of the shower that had been "repaired" with a garbage bag and some duct tape. You had to kick the front door to get in and out. They primarily used plastic plates and utensils to eat off. The dog dish was so dirty it made my skin crawl. It was a living nightmare. I am shuddering just writing about it! So, what was his deal? This was a man raised with a scarcity mindset who had stayed there. A man who made good money, and spent it on things like thick gold chains, but didn't feel deserving of a nice (or even clean) home. A man whose identity was totally about struggle.

Some people are a blessing, and some people are a lesson. But let's leave these men alone and take responsibility and ownership for the only piece of it that I can: myself.

I say this as bluntly as I can: what in the sweet tootin' tarnation was I doing getting involved with these men?

It was all an indication of my standards, and what I believed was possible. As a self-proclaimed weirdo, I had been looking for love that met "weirdo" criteria.

It was as if I had a checklist:

♥ Are you a bit weird?
♥ Do you dress a bit weird?
♥ Do you make me laugh?

Okay, let's go!

Maybe some of this was borne from early pain, where "normal" people had never been that interested in me, and because of that rejection, my subconscious mind had decided that weirdos and outsiders were going to cause less pain.

A lot of us have created our desires as a way of escaping hurt. We want this because it doesn't remind us of that. We only want people with these characteristics because people with *those* qualities have hurt us deeply in the past.

It's so important that we really take stock of who we are attracting and why. This is one reason why journaling can be such a powerful tool: it gives us time and space to meander and think about why we have made the choices of our lives.

Because my only real criteria was "Are you a bit weird?" I then ended up dealing with all kinds of things that I hadn't even thought about.

Sure, my partners were weird, funny and smart. But they were also struggling with... * Chronic depression * Substance abuse * Traumatic childhoods * PTSD * Crippling debt * Lack of ambition * Self-deception * Suicidal thoughts * Resentment and bitterness... And the list goes on.

Now, none of those things make you a bad person. Most of us have experienced these things at one time or another! But if you are depressed or suicidal and you're not doing anything about it? Not going to therapy, not taking medication, not meditating, not tapping, not taking any steps towards healing, resolution or personal responsibility? We're gonna have a problem. And I say WE because YOUR problems become MY problems.

This relationship stuff is not trivial. The person you choose to mate with, live with, marry, or spend exorbitant amounts of time with better be the absolute best person *you can find*. Because their standards will become your own. Their interests will permeate your life. Their friends will become your friends. And if you hate their standards, their interests bore you senseless, and you'd rather jump out a window than talk to their bestie... You are setting yourself up for a life of misery.

In addition to creating a life with someone who inspires you, makes you want to be a better human, and holds you in high regard, one of your other essential considerations should be avoiding anything that is going to snuff out your light.

If you think this job, that partner, this city, or having a baby might snuff out your light? *Run as far as you can in the other direction.*

Your light is the most important thing that you possess, and yet it is hard to describe. It is your spark, your glee, your euphoric edge. It's the piece of you that sparkles with childlike joy, it's what you tap into when you share your love with your best friends, it is the source of all your creativity. Your light helps you to see the world as a beautiful place, spilling over with excitement and opportunities and new ideas.

And when your light gets dimmed by a living situation, a lover, a soul-sucking career? I know that you know how that feels. I know that you know what it looks like. It looks and feels gray, hopeless, depressing and frustrated.

And I also know that you know how it feels when you *let* go of whatever has been dimming you for so long! When you leave that city, that job, that relationship... Your radiance turns up to 11 and you are in living color once more. You feel supersonic. The world is full of glory. Nothing is impossible and you savor the juiciness of life like it's the most delicious tropical smoothie.

The most important thing in life is that YOU NEVER DIM YOUR LIGHT.

So here's what this means, in a romantic context.

It means that if they bore you on your first date, you politely say you're not interested in seeing them again.

It means that if she acts unreasonably jealous or can't be happy for your successes, you cut her off.

It means that you stay far, far away from anyone who makes you feel like you have to be someone else... Or constantly defend your own behavior.

It also means that you stop making excuses for everyone else. We *all* had messed-up childhoods. The real question is: are you doing the work, or are you simply repeating cycles?

And this may mean that you spend big chunks of time single. But I move that relationships only have VALUE when they are EXCEPTIONAL. When the person we are with is elevating us (and vice versa), when they bring massive amounts of fun, joy and adventure to our lives, when we are mutually worshiping one another!

If a relationship is not bringing you these things, it is just another job. Another thing you have to manage. Another distraction in this world which is already trying to distract us in a million other ways!

It is infinitely better to be *absolutely single*—and free, joyful, productive and creative—than to be in a relationship that makes you want to sleep all day.

Now, if this is ringing very, very true for you, please don't feel that I am in attack mode. I am writing this as much for myself as I am for you! This is a place where we can very easily slip up. I mean, just look at your parents' relationship(s). What did you truly learn that was of value there? Okay, I rest my case!

We don't know how to do this. And I see so many books on how to make relationships work, but so *few* on choosing someone who is really going to raise you up! Why struggle and take seminars and see a therapist to make a relationship work with someone who really, truly, you know, deep down, is not capable of meeting you at your highest potential?

I want you to take a mental inventory right now of all the things that you bring to the table. And if you're struggling, call up your best friend and ask them, "Hey. What do you think I'm like as a romantic partner? What do I bring to the table?" Then take notes. I promise, it will blow your mind. It will make you see yourself *very differently.*

You have all these incredible things going on. All these skills and qualities that anyone would be so *delighted* to be around. And yet, we are sitting around hoping to be picked by someone who—let's face it—nine times out of ten doesn't have HALF of the qualities we already possess!

Then we think that we have to perform and live up to some ridiculous standard in order to "attract a mate" who is oftentimes bringing very little to the table! It's sheer insanity.

Trust me when I say it is so much better to be single, love yourself radically, and live your juiciest life than be with someone who drags you down every day.

And the coolest part about it is that when you really are living that divine, guided, juicy life… The perfect partner will just show up.

THIRTY NON-NEGOTIABLE QUALITIES

I was talking to my friend Jerico Mandybur about her love life. She just got married and is so happy, and as someone who is fascinated by romantic relationships, I asked her about the journey she'd undertaken to get there.

Jerico told me that she had been dilly-dallying around with low standards, dating people who, quite simply, were not what she was looking for. Because her standards were so low, a friend of hers challenged her to write a list of 30 qualities that she was looking for in a partner. Jerico thought, 'Damn! I don't even know if I can think of that many!' and that very thought inspired her to write the list.

Some of the things on the list were major, and some were minor. Once she'd written it, she sat back and thought, 'Well, hell. I don't even embody all of these qualities!' It felt like a major wake-up call, and as a result, she started to work on them, little by little. Improving herself every day.

Shortly after that, she met her partner. And her partner possesses ALL THIRTY OF THESE QUALITIES.

Take that one to the bank next time someone tells you that your high standards are going to result in spinster status!

Just like my friend Jerico, I'd like you to make a list of 30 qualities that are essential to you in a partner. And I want you to do this *no matter* whether you are single, in a relationship, married, or not even looking. It is a fantastic mental exercise that will bring you so much clarity.

Get cozy, light some candles, and start writing your list. As you do it, think back over partners you've had in the past. What did you love, and what did you loathe? What are your absolute non-negotiables?

At least now you have a yardstick! And don't feel bad for having suffered in shoddy, frustrating, or unfulfilling relationships for so long. It wasn't for nought if you learned something. Every crappy relationship or miserable partner gives us the gift of clarity... As you hopefully remember from Chapter Three!

EMBODYING YOUR OWN 30 QUALITIES

Here's the part that so many of us miss: we want a partner with all these incredible qualities, but we forget that *we need to embody them too.*

Why? Why can't we just rely on someone else to bring us everything that we want and desire?

Firstly, that is an unreal burden. Imagine if you met someone who just sat back and demanded things of you that they were totally unwilling to do themselves. You would be so aggravated, and there's no way you would stick around! It's not fair to ask things of people that you wouldn't do yourself.

Secondly, it places your power outside of yourself. If you rely on someone else to do this or that, you are giving all of your power away, subjugating yourself, and acting as if you are not a goddess. You can do, be and have anything—remember?!

I was talking to a friend of mine about this recently. She met a man while she was still in college, moved in with him, and let him run the show until she was in her mid-thirties. When they split up, she was terrified. She didn't know how to find an apartment, set up an internet connection, or pay her bills. The good news is that she figured it out... And now loves being single and independent!

However, she spent a huge chunk of her life relying on and depending upon this man, and not in a way that felt good. It felt disempowering and scary for her.

So often, we are asking others to be and do for us things that we are not willing to be and do for ourselves.

When you hear phrases like "Be your own lover," this is exactly what is being talked about. Being your own lover is not about just enjoying time alone—it is about embodying the qualities and traits, and even learning the skills, that you hope for in another person.

For example, you may want your lover to be an unbelievably encouraging cheerleader, who tells you you're always doing a great job. But if you are not able to do this for yourself, you are putting an enormous burden on them. They will begin to feel responsible for cheering you on, which—quite frankly—is not their job! Not to mention, all the compliments and encouragement in the world don't make a dent if *you don't believe them*. You have to be your own biggest cheerleader first!

As you can see, writing down these thirty qualities is not some trivial assignment. It is actually a roadmap for who you want to be.

Some of these skills or qualities can be picked up in 21 days. Others will take a longer time to master, but wow, imagine the journey and personal growth you'll experience as you work on them! And maybe you will never be able to tick off all thirty, but maybe, just maybe, you will! Wouldn't that be incredible? To be your own dream?!

Thirdly, from an energetic standpoint, the closer you can move to being your own version of abundance realized, the easier it will be to attract people who are in that same lane. They will be drawn to you, because you are radiating the same stuff they are radiating. If you only possess one of those thirty qualities you're looking for, your vibration is *completely* different than theirs!

MARRIAGE IS NOT AN ACHIEVEMENT

Here's a reminder: marriage is not an achievement.

This is something we need to be reminded of *all the time* because our culture forces this idea down our throats. Society shouts at women: your wedding is "your day!" The day that you get all eyes on you! The day that you are truly validated! Hooray, you have finally been picked! You are good enough! Release the doves!

But... A wedding is just a party. Whether you have one, eight (like Elizabeth Taylor), or nine weddings (like Zsa-Zsa Gabor), it shouldn't affect your self-esteem or your self-worth. And so often we get fixated on the idea of a wedding—which lasts eight hours if you're lucky—as opposed to a marriage—which is supposed to last forever.

When I got married, I did it for the wrong reasons. I did it because I was 27, and I was in love, and I just thought, 'This is what people do.' Looking back on it, I simply do not believe this is a good enough reason to commit to someone for life.

So many women get married because they feel like they should, that it's time, their parents or family are pressuring them, they're desperate to have a baby, they're worried no one else will ask, or they're afraid of saying no and what the alternatives might be.

The number of women I see in sad marriages is truly heartbreaking. And even worse than that are the excuses they use to justify them. "He's not so bad... At least I love my friends!... It's better than what my parents had... We've been together so long I wouldn't know what to do... I don't know how to leave... I'm afraid to be by myself... At least I have wine! Lol!"

Can we please make a pact? Can we please swear to DO BETTER for ourselves than this?

When my marriage was on the rocks, I knew that it needed to end, but I just didn't have the courage to pull the trigger. I was on my way to Tulum, for an astrology retreat no less, and I remember thinking to myself, 'On this trip, I want a sign about what I should do.' Well, wouldn't you know? Absolutely *every single woman* attending the retreat was divorced... And I had never seen a happier group of people!

Baby, if you are in a happy relationship, you can ignore this! I'm delighted for you and I hope you are too! But this section is for the people who swore "'Til death do us part" and feel like something is missing. Society tells us that marriage is the norm, something everyone should do. I don't believe anything is universally the "right thing" for everyone! The sheer delight pouring out of the women at the retreat in Tulum was evidence enough!

Maybe some people shouldn't get married. Maybe some people shouldn't have children. Is that so awful? Think about the adventures, the wild love affairs, the way you could decorate your home! Think of the disposable income! Oh my god, it's enough to make you froth at the mouth with pure delight!

What is so terrible about being single? Absolutely nothing!

We are groomed to believe that being married is the pinnacle of human achievement. Well, for women anyway. (Don't get me started.) But don't be fooled! It comes with some significant challenges.

This is not to say that you should avoid relationships and marriage entirely. What I am saying is that if this is a path you choose to traverse, you better do it with someone who is worth your time!

Please do not invest your time and energy into someone who cannot even do the dishes, clip their toenails, or contribute in any real way.

Here's the good news: it is never too late to completely switch it up. It is never too late to change your beliefs. It is never too late to tell yourself a new story. In fact, you've already started!

BE RESPONSIBLE WITH YOUR ENERGY

You may not be aware of this, but you are a very bright light. Right now, these may just be words to you, but I know, in time, you will truly grasp this notion.

It's true. You are incandescent. This took me a long time understand, even for myself. I am bright, baby! The longer you exist in the world, the more you realize how truly different and wonderful you are. If you are reading this, you are right there with me. I know it for a fact.

It is fabulous to be this way. It is fantastic to be able to generate your own light, and to have such attractive energy. At the same time, it comes with its own issues. When you are like this—and you are—it is also your *responsibility* to remember that the light draws in a lot of people.

When you are a person who feels good a lot of the time, people cannot help but be curious. Do you find you are always making random friends at the coffee shop, or people love to strike up conversations with you? That's because of your light, honey!

My friend has a joke that people like you and me are our own planets, with their own gravitational pull, and we have many moons circling around us at all times. These moons are the people who are drawn in. Many people will be attracted to you because they are like-hearted, some will be drawn in because they are dark. They feel lost. They feel stuck. And they could use a little bit of your light.

Have you ever experienced this before? Where you suddenly look around and a lot of your friends—or lovers—are in crisis? Or you realize that *all your lovers* have been in crisis?!

Here's the real truth. If you know that your energy is addictive, it is up to you to create boundaries.

It is up to you to say no. It is up to you to walk away. It is up to you to decline the call, unfollow the account, hit the block button.

Is this hard sometimes? Absolutely! Especially when you can see the potential in someone, or you love them. But is it essential to do this in order to preserve your own light? One trillion percent.

MAYBE IN THE PAST, BUT TRY ME TODAY

We know exactly who people are as soon as we meet them. Your intuition is never off. As soon as you see or talk to someone new, you get a sense or a feeling about them. When you think back on it, after maybe months or even years have passed, weren't your first impressions always right? It's incredible what we have allowed in our lives—and I include myself in this statement!

I remember going on a first date and being immediately put off. It was lunch, and when I showed up, he was sitting inside... With his sunglasses on. He kept them on for almost the entire meal. Now, I have nothing against sunglasses—in fact, they are one of my favorite things to buy. But wearing them during a meal... Inside?! What are you trying to hide? What are you so afraid of?

During that meal, our conversation was totally weird. We didn't connect at all! He talked a lot and none of his jokes made me laugh. And when we went to say goodbye, there was no hug or any kind of affection. Imagine my surprise when he *shook* my hand before skateboarding off into the distance!

It was one of the weirdest first dates I'd had up until that point. I wrote him off completely. But when he invited me out dancing a couple of nights later, and the drinks started flowing... All bets were off. We ended up together for two years! And yes, this is the man whose floor was so filthy I always wanted to wear a pair of socks!

He and I were not a match, and you must remember that you are massively influenced by whoever is around you. His internal belief systems of struggle and hardship started to become a part of my identity too. No big surprise, then, that when we broke up, my business absolutely exploded and has been constantly abundant ever since!

So let this be a lesson to you. If you meet someone and you have a funny feeling about them, *honor that feeling!* All sorts of people will be drawn to you, but it is up to you to have boundaries and say no.

I remember once going out on a date with a man who was nice, but with whom I had zero chemistry. The next day, I texted him to say I had a lovely time but thought we would be better as friends. He texted me back and asked if we could "debrief"—yes, he was a Capricorn!—and when I got on the phone with him, I told him that I hadn't felt a spark.

"Oh," he said. "I'm not sure if I felt a spark or not... I was attracted to you so sometimes that blocks out knowing whether I can feel a spark."

This is *precisely* my point! If you go out with someone, it is very likely that they are so dazzled by you, you little minx, that they can't tell their ass from their elbow! (This is the blessing and the curse of being so incredible.) It is up to YOU to feel it out, and act accordingly.

If you want to know whether you've grown, travel back in your mind to some of those people you've dated in the past. Without knowing where things would go, and purely based on their behavior on a first date, if you met them today, would you have said yes to a second date? In fact, you might not have even given them your number when they first approached you!

We are constantly honing our instincts and our intuition, and we are gaining more clarity with every passing day. So in this way, we are always growing, improving and reaching for more.

The men from my past have been such huge lessons for me, both in showing me what I *don't* want, and in the gifts they gave me, because I truly can look in the rearview mirror and see what I gained from each relationship. Thankfully though, I will never go backwards to be with someone like them ever again. Onwards and upwards, baby!

The point is that we have to make some mistakes—aka experience some resistance, aka learn some lessons—in order to get clarity around what we want going forward. If I hadn't had relationships where I experienced this or that, I wouldn't have known so vehemently what I truly desired, and I wouldn't have that clarity as fuel to get me to my next situation.

It's all a blessing. And it always turns out for the best.

DON'T MAKE EXCUSES FOR OTHER PEOPLE

"If you have a relationship with someone who does not love himself or herself, then it is impossible to really please that person. You will never be good enough for someone who is insecure, frustrated, jealous, self-loathing, or resentful. Too often we knock ourselves out trying to be good enough for partners who don't have any idea

how to accept our love, because they don't love who they are."
—Louise Hay

It's wonderful to be understanding, to be able to listen, and to really empathize with others. These are fantastic skills to have, but sometimes we end up using them against ourselves.

When you are an empathetic person, one of the greatest dangers you face is that you have the ability to excuse all manner of terrible behavior because you understand where it came from. When someone does something you don't like, you might be mad, but you may also find yourself thinking, 'But with a childhood like that, what else could I expect? He's doing the best that he can! Bless him.'

Other ways that we excuse other people's behavior may include...

- ♥ "But she's a Scorpio!"
- ♥ "But it's Mercury retrograde."
- ♥ "But he didn't feel attractive when he was growing up, of course he needs to flirt now and make up for it."
- ♥ "But she promised she'll change. I believe her."

Does this sound familiar? If it does, I implore you to *stop making excuses for other people.*

It's so easy to do this. To explain away the bad behavior. To defend your heartache. To be so sweet and understanding that *you end up missing out on your life.*

All that time spent defending someone else's behavior, trying to understand them (especially when they don't give you the same grace) or tip-toeing around, trying not to piss them off, could be spent in a million other ways. It could be spent alone, working on creative projects, and building your skills. It could be spent in another relationship, with someone who has a great personality and doesn't make excuses, just does better. The choices are endless. But you simply don't have to stay in something that doesn't feel good.

In fact, when we do this to ourselves—when we stay, even when we know it isn't right—we are simply doing mental gymnastics because our fear of being alone is so high.

Most people are doing their best. But to be brutally honest, their best may not be good enough if *you* want to be exceptional. Only you can decide that for yourself.

Please understand that *you cannot heal another person.* It is up to your partner to do that for themselves. They are the ones who need to do plant medicine in the jungle, start meditating, or unpacking their childhood with an unwavering eye.

You cannot do it for them. If they are unwilling to do this, they will pass their unresolved trauma onto you... And then it becomes your problem.

You cannot love someone into changing.

As someone who is doing the work, you can only be with people who are also doing the work. On their own. Unprompted. Truly.

Being alone is not a punishment or a curse. It is a gift. If you can view it through the right lens, your solitude will lead you to some of the best times of your life. Being single—by choice!—doesn't mean there is anything wrong with you, or that you are flawed, or that you are not deserving of love. It simply means that you prioritize *yourself* more than your desire to be in a relationship with anyone who gives you a wink.

Now, don't get me wrong. I am all about beautiful, delicious, romantic love. And I believe that the highest ideal for a romantic relationship is one of unconditional love. But I also believe that we need to be extremely selective about who we enter into these relationships with! Not everyone is deserving of everything you have to give.

EXPAND YOUR ROMANTIC VISIONS

In the past, I chronically limited my vision of what love could be. My desires were small. And as you know by now, if you have small dreams, you get small rewards. I wanted to be in love. I wanted to have sex. I wanted to be married, I suppose! Done, done, and done. Easy. But what if my dreams had been bigger?

What if my visions had been epic? What if I was aflame for deep soul connection and never ending passion? What if I had wanted, like Elizabeth Taylor, to be lavished with jewels from my admirers? What if I had envisioned a life of extreme service and equally extreme joy and abundance, like Tony and Sage Robbins?

There are absolutely no limits to how incredible your life can be, and this is doubly true when it comes to your relationships. After all, adding someone else into your manifestations can either turn them supersonic... Or crush them just as quickly.

One thing I've learned is that a team gets things done much more quickly than a single person. Many hands make light work, and when many souls are enthusiastic about something, it takes off!

The same is true of partnership. The right partner can see you as you are now but can also see how much better it could be, how much further you could go. They can work alongside you to craft a delicious vision that blows both your minds, and then commit to making it happen. You can truly work magic together, and sharing success with someone that you love is one of the best feelings in the world.

But the wrong partner? The wrong partner will suppress you, make you doubt yourself, keep you on a hamster wheel of drama, burden you with their unresolved trauma, and—to put it plainly—waste your time.

The worst part is that we can't even BLAME THEM! We can only point the finger at ourselves for having let them slip past, undetected. For not dreaming bigger for ourselves. For allowing ourselves to squander our time. For not saying no when we felt that little feeling inside that said, 'This is a red flag.'

So how can we raise our romantic standards?

Start seeking out stories of love that make you feel good. There are *lots* of them. Watch romantic comedies and feel them in your body. Do some research on couples that have love you'd like to emulate. And stop spending time with— or following on social media!—people who complain about whichever gender you're most attracted to. Write that list of thirty qualities and start embodying them yourself.

A while ago, I asked a friend of mine how his love life was going.

"Still looking for my queen. We shall see. Sometimes I think I'm asking for too much, but I damn sure don't wanna settle," he said.

"It's never asking too much when you are living the traits that you want in someone else," I replied. "And you are."

Because he is! He is looking for a confident, magnetic, spiritual woman who practices what she preaches... And that is exactly what he is. I am sure that she is closer than he even thinks! Maybe one day she will unroll her yoga mat next to his and he will *just know!*

The truth is that the more that you EMBODY the qualities you find attractive, the more you will know it is POSSIBLE to find that in somebody else. And the more you will draw in like-minded—or like-hearted—people.

YOU GET IT BY NOT NEEDING IT

Hopefully, I am sending a clear message to you: love is wonderful, *and* we need to be extremely picky.

After all, you are picky about how you dress, the car you drive, and how you decorate your home. You do the best you can with what you've got! You're even picky about what you put on your Instagram feed! Shouldn't the process of choosing a partner be at least as rigorous?!

My experience has been that in order to attract a *healthy* relationship—by which I mean one in which two people are living happy, independent lives, and not looking to others to prop up their faltering self-esteem—we have to let go of any desperation around wanting one.

When I think back on all the times a romance flourished in my life, it is almost like my joy at being single watered the seeds of romance. We all know how very unattractive it is when anyone is desperate for anything. In fact, if you go on a first date, and you can't stop yourself from talking about how badly you want to be married with children, you can almost guarantee that your paramour will run a mile!

So how do we take the edge off? How do we reduce the urgency and sense of rising panic?

RADICAL SELF-LOVE, BABY! Double-down on your single life and *love it* as if it could be ripped away from you tomorrow. Because, plot twist, it could be!

I know that can feel difficult, especially when you're in a place where you're walking around, wishing, hoping, and praying to be snuggled up with some particular cutie. But I am telling you, the more time you take with yourself, and the more you invest in making your life really, really fun, the faster those cravings will subside.

Fill your life with whatever makes you feel good. Go absolutely wild with it! Find clubs, classes and groups in your area and fill your calendar! Make friends and laugh with them late into the night. Trust me, you won't enjoy being single if you're sitting around alone bored all the time!

I fill my life with workouts (I'm a nerd, it's honestly one of my favorite things to do), bike rides, kickboxing, Pilates, and dance class. I go to art shows with friends, decorate my house, write books, film videos, record podcasts, read in bed, take long beach walks, go shopping, travel, laugh my ass off with my best friends, go to comedy shows, concerts, find cute coffee shops, take day trips... The list is endless!

When you make your single life so much fun, you raise your barometer for the people who want to walk into your life. This way, if you're talking to some potential suitor about going out and you think you'd have a better time by yourself, it's easy to turn them down! Your life should be so lush and juicy that an interested party has to really, really bring something exceptional to the table. You don't want to be lonely and bored, sitting around your house, waiting for the phone to ring. Your day should be action-packed, fun and full of laughter, and by the time you go to bed, you should be absolutely exhausted!

It might feel, right now, like having a lover in your life will fill all those emotional holes you have. And when you meet your next beloved, it will feel great for a little while! But eventually, those dizzying feelings will wear off, and you will be with yourself again, even if you're still together! If you haven't worked on loving yourself and your own company, you will start to think there is something wrong with your relationship... When really, the problem is that you are not comfortable with yourself.

The real work is in healing yourself, and loving yourself wholeheartedly, without needing anything external to shine you up. There's no getting away from it: it always comes back to radical self-love!

YOUR TIME AND ENERGY ARE PRECIOUS

Let me drive this point home, just quickly, because it's easy to forget.

If you are making time for someone else, that is an HONOR. Whoever is fortunate enough to have caught your eye should be *delighted* that you are even giving them the time of day. Phew!

Honey, think of all the other things you could be doing with your time: building your empire, making piles of money, laughing with your friends, taking a class, reading poetry, having multiple orgasms, napping, getting a massage... The list goes on.

Make no mistake, when you are spending time with someone, you are not doing something else. You have to ask yourself, 'Is this really worth it?'

WHAT ARE YOU WILLING TO PUT UP WITH?

Let's say that you have just started dating someone. They make your heart beat faster, you think about them all day long, and the sex is out of this world. What could be better? N-o-t-h-i-n-g. You're making all your friends sick by constantly talking about this person. It's one of the greatest feelings in the world.

I know you're in a love haze, and I want you to enjoy it! But I also want you to pay attention. People show you who they are without even meaning to, and in these first couple of months, you are getting a taste of who they really are.

In the beginning, your new lover is showing you their very best representative. You're not yet entirely comfortable with each other, so they are really doing everything they can to be awesome. (And you are too!) So while you're both in this period, you have to be observant and look at what they're showing you.

Make no mistake, everyone comes to the table with their own cornucopia full of issues. Everyone. But the question is, what issues are you willing to put up with... And which issues are going to elicit a *hard pass*?

Pay attention to what they are saying or doing. Listen to the content of their jokes. (There is almost always an element of truth to them!) If you're only a month in and they're displaying bad behavior—like a nasty temper, deep intolerance, jealousy, or rudeness—I know it might be hard, but take note and get out of there!

If it makes you uncomfortable now, it is not going to get any better.

Please know that it is not your "karma" to be with a difficult partner. You have no obligation to saddle up beside them while they work their life out. What they are showing you, right now, today, is who they are.

Let me say that again. THIS IS WHO THEY ARE, *especially* if they're displaying it in the beginning, when they are actually still showing you their best possible self!

So it is essential that you ask yourself: is this something I really want to deal with?! Is the trade of my time, energy, and effort worth what I am getting in return?

CLEARING YOUR LOVE BLOCKS

Let's say that you're single and loving it. Hooray! Good for you! But you still think it would be lovely to be in a relationship. I don't blame you!

In that case, it is important to clear out any resistance you may have around finding love. One of the biggest blockages to love is not a sense of unworthiness or a feeling of despair, although of course those are very powerful and will certainly keep love at a distance. No, one of the most potent blocks is a feeling of *jealousy*. Specifically, jealousy when our friends seem to have found love and we haven't!

Jealousy can crop up when we least expect it, and it is always circling around a locus of fear and scarcity-based thinking. When we fall into jealousy, it is because, at some unconscious level, we are afraid that if it happens for someone else, maybe there are less opportunities for us. If a friend of yours gets into a relationship, we can feel jealous because we fear that the relationship will take their love, time, and attention away from us.

This is all quite normal and okay. Remember the tapping mantra: Even though [I feel jealous], I deeply and completely love, and accept, and forgive myself! You can tap on this yourself, any time it comes up!

I have found that the best antidote to jealousy is to instead trust in the timing of the universe. Rather than going down the rabbit-hole of "Why her and why not me?" decide to flip that in your mind! Instead, choose to believe that the universe's timing is absolutely perfect.

Sure, your friend may have fallen in love, and you are still lying on the couch, swiping through the dating apps. But maybe the reason for that is because the Universe is cooking up your perfect match. Maybe she was more aligned to her match, and you still have some vibrational work to do!

And maybe this is simply the right time for you to be single. Perhaps there are things you need to learn: about being alone, about not using romantic attention as validation, about self-esteem, about the power of friendship. Maybe you just need this time to get truly clear on what it is you want. Maybe there's another project that requires your attention right now. Maybe you need this time to heal.

CAN A SITUATIONSHIP BE HIGH VIBE?

You might be surprised at my answer, but I believe a situationship—as in, something sexual but not serious—can be totally high vibe. In fact, it can even reset your frequency!

I've had two times in my life where a big relationship ended and, before I got into my next serious moment, I had fun in a situationship which also helped me work through some old energetic stuff.

As a card-carrying Virgo, I sure do love my opposite sign of Pisces. Is it any wonder, then, that these two situationships involved Pisces men? Two different Pisces, mind you, on two different coasts!

Both of these Pisces are truly good men. They live to please. They just wanted to make me feel good. And they were both able to be involved, and stay relaxed while also being respectful. That's a beautiful dance. In fact, I think of both of these men as my "Pisces palate cleansers!"

When I think back to the first Pisces, it is only ever with warmth and affection. We had a great few months where we would hang out every week, listen to music, and have amazing sex. When I consider the greater context of my life, it is *so clear to me* that he was part of my journey. In many ways, he helped me cope with the dissolution of my previous relationship by being, well, pretty much the total opposite of my ex. And he helped me get ready for my next one by reminding me that I was hot, and fun, and a catch!

The next Pisces did absolutely the same thing, except in an even lovelier way. (Was our entanglement better because of him, or because I had evolved so much? Probably a bit of both.) With Pisces #2, I began to unlock parts of myself that I didn't even know existed. He helped me see myself in a totally new way. And in between all of those moments, we made each other laugh, went to comedy clubs, ate dessert in bed, and cuddled.

Situationships like these play a huge role in our healing. Sometimes relationships end badly, or when they do finally come to a close, you realize how toxic they truly were. The people that come along after that can be true angels, with the power to restore your sense of self and help you remember how incredible you are.

These situationships can prepare you for the next big love. I think about flings like this as really good vibrational practice. After all, anything you can do to feel good and feel the way you want to feel is good for you! So embrace situationships, as long as they are fun and uplifting! In the best ones, you will remember what great sex feels like, you will remember what it feels like to be cared for, you will remember what it is like to see someone who puts a smile on your face. All of these things are valuable and lovely.

The very best situationships can also inspire you to uplevel in a serious way. If you were in a relationship where the sex was depressing, it is so powerful to begin experiencing true sexual compatibility, a sense of play and adventure, and feeling lust again! In addition to it being great vibrational practice, it is good *physical* practice too.

Maybe your next situationship will feel so good and comfortable that you will discover totally new things about your sexual appetite... And that will prepare you for your next great love. Remember, it is all working out in the way that it is supposed to! Always!

IF YOU'VE BEEN DUMPED

I know it hurts. Believe me. But remember, everything is happening for you, and not to you.

Truly, this is a gift.

If you have been dumped or rejected, if your love has been unrequited, if you are separated or divorced... GOD BLESS. Blow that person kisses in your mind every single day.

Maybe you didn't want this to happen, and I promise, I feel your pain. But this other person has done you a massive service. They have forced you to double-down on *yourself*, freed you to pursue something even better, released you from their burdens and troubles.

I remember going through a pretty bad break-up and waking up the next morning. As sad as I felt, I also recall being extremely aware that the anxiety I had been carrying for such a long time had *entirely lifted*. The anxiety I had been feeling was not mine: it had been a side-effect of being with this person and trying to make something that was wrong feel *right*.

When we are in relationships with other people, and especially when we are having sex with and sleeping beside them, our energies are constantly mingling. This is why it is *so important* to choose the right person to get involved with.

If someone has left you, abandoned you, rejected you, ask yourself, 'What have I gained?' I promise you, there are plenty of gifts in their absence. At the very least, now you have much more spare time. How delicious. Now the only question left to ask is what you're going to do with all this freedom!

When something comes to an end, I am almost always struck with a realization of my true worth. As I move forward and think about what I want next, it becomes very clear to me where I was not getting all of my needs met. This is almost always a place where I realize that I have been playing too small or safe, or tolerating something that would no longer be acceptable to me. When you are able to look at your life objectively, endings can be very powerful, positive, and useful!

STAR-CROSS'D LOVERS

What can you do if you're ready, but the person you really like is not? My suggestion is to gently pry your hands off the wheel and relax. While this might feel painful, confusing, aggravating, and a whole other host of emotions, *we cannot do anything to make another person ready for our brilliance.*

Some people will never be able to handle you at your most radiant. In that case, they are really and truly doing you a favor by refusing to step up to the plate. If they aren't able to match your energy, your relationship will be full of resistance, otherwise known as pain.

Some people have their own stuff to work on, and if you want to remain in their life while they do so, that's okay. Be a friend and be supportive. That's a beautiful thing to do. But make sure you are not doing it at the cost of your own sanity or joy, and make sure you are not dulling your light in order to remain a friend.

If an almost-relationship is causing you pain (which primarily happens because you are focusing on the absence of what you want, rather than the abundance of what you already have), then it's important to either change your perspective or step away.

You cannot and should not put your life on hold while someone you love sorts through their feelings. Because even though you are a shooting star, a glorious marvel, a delicious morsel, they might not ever be able to see it. Or maybe they see it, but they are afraid. These things are not your fault.

So if you want to be their friend, that's lovely—but make sure you are still living your life. Keep going on dates. Keep exploring the world.

I truly believe that when people are meant for each other, the Universe will conspire to make that happen. They will turn up again when you least expect it, or they will approach you out of the blue. Nothing that is for you will pass you!

There is no way to force this or speed up the process, other than digging deep into your own life to discover what beauty you can create and experience.

The answer to all of life's questions is always more *radical self-love!*

HOW TO LET IT GO

One of the most crucial places we get tripped up is in our lack of forgiveness for the past. It is essential that we are able to let bygones be bygones. You cannot drag around rage or toxicity around a past relationship and expect to attract a healthy partner. No—it's much more likely that you will draw in someone who is in a similar emotional place to you.

Sometimes we get forgiveness twisted, as we assume that it means that we are condoning the behavior of the other person. Forgiveness is not something that we do for the other person, it is something we do for our own grace. It is about letting ourselves off the hook, putting down our own bag of rocks.

The angrier we are about situations from our past, the harder it is to move on.

Tapping is a very effective way to help move yourself towards forgiveness. There are a lot of tapping for forgiveness videos on YouTube, and Brad Yates is one of my favorite people to tap along with. Don't just tap to forgive the other person, tap to forgive yourself, too. Forgive yourself for being involved, for turning a blind eye, for not listening to your intuition, for staying too long. Whatever it is that turns your stomach when you think about it, tap on it! This will radically change your energy around love and relationships!

Another way to experience a sense of forgiveness is to try to look at whatever the situation gave you that was positive. This might be hard, especially if this person or relationship was the source of a lot of pain, but no matter how terrible the situation, you definitely gained *something* from your interaction with them!

Maybe you gained greater empathy for women who have been in similar situations. Maybe your ex taught you how not to manage your money! Maybe they taught you what to look out for in the future. Despite the pain, all of those things are gifts.

To move out of victimhood, we need to look at how our past has served us. What has it taught us? What has it coaxed out of us? How has it made us stronger, smarter and more determined? How has it encouraged us to raise our standards?

These can be hard questions to ask ourselves, and sometimes we are reticent to attribute anything positive to a person who was so destructive. But doing this is not, in any way, saying that what this person did was okay or that you would get involved with them again. Instead, it is a way of taking ownership of our lives and using all of our past experiences as fuel. Taking the pain and transforming it into something useful! Something that propels us into the future, feeling proud of ourselves, as we leave shame in the dust.

Shame is such a limiting emotion. It makes us want to shrink ourselves, play small, and keeps us stuck and afraid. It prevents us from moving into new situations that could be so positive! It stops us from taking risks, because we are too busy beating ourselves up and being disappointed in our behavior from the past.

The truth is that we can only do things to the best of our given ability at any moment. Maybe you needed to have this or that experience in order to discover what you will never tolerate again. And here's the best thing: now that you know better, you can do better! You will. And you are.

HOW DO WE REALLY FIND LOVE?

I made a joke the other day that the subtitle of this book should have been "How To Get Everything By Not Wanting Anything At All."

This is the great lesson of manifesting: it is only when you let it go that it comes. It is only when you walk away that they run after you. This is not coincidence: it is that you dropped your attachment to needing that thing. You released your resistance. You woke up one day and realized you didn't need it. You turned away, fell in love with yourself. And suddenly, the thing you wanted is available to you.

This is just as true when it comes to relationships. You have let go of the desire in order to receive it.

How do we manifest love?

We stop thinking about it. We fill our lives with so much joy that we don't even have time to miss it. We settle comfortably into the knowledge that we are not missing out on anything, and that when the time is right, an incredible person will show up. And we trust the divine timing of the universe.

But the biggest secret to finding a healthy relationship is to double-down on radical self-love. To be so deeply joyful at the idea of having a weekend to yourself, without responsibilities or obligations, that any desperation or need is completely obliterated.

It is my secret magical wish that reading this chapter will kick you out of your desire for love... So that it can come to you!

Let me know how it works out! ✳

08

LOVING IN
THE VORTEX

W E'VE NOW TALKED AT LENGTH ABOUT THE NEED to raise our standards so that we can attract a partner that is truly *worthy* of our energetic investment. For many of you, the last chapter simply reaffirmed what you already knew: that you are in a beautiful, healthy partnership. Yes babe, yes!

Manifesting consists of a few distinct pieces. There's the journey towards getting what you desire, there's the getting of it, and then there's the ultimate trick: maintaining the sweetness. One of the most challenging places to do this can be within your relationship, because it's not just you!

Here are some essential tips to keep your love life sweet and satisfying.

ALWAYS DO YOUR BEST

In a relationship, you are constantly being faced with the reality that *you cannot control another person.* Your job, your health and your finances are a little more self-contained. If you don't like how things are going, you have absolute autonomy and there are so many ways to change an outcome. But in a relationship? Isn't it different?

Well, yes. And no!

If you do at the end of a relationship what you did at the start, there will never be an end.

You can never control another person. But you can control *yourself.* You can ensure that you are pouring the highest levels of energy into the relationship. You can learn new skills, become a better communicator, and be attentive, and all of these things will improve your relationship.

The truth about love is that there are no guarantees, and there is really no security. Your beloved could walk into a supermarket tomorrow and fall in love with someone handling a piece of filet mignon. *You never know!* They might wake up one day and change their mind, decide they want something different, or— and this is a big one—feel unworthy of your love, and thus sabotage it. But even if they do these things, if you give the relationship 100% of what you are capable of, at least you will know that you did your best.

Other than pouring into the relationship, it is essential that our sense of self-love is so strong that we feel good about the way we're showing up. When you love yourself and the way you engage with the world, it stamps out your insecurities. It also means that someone changing their mind about you doesn't feel personal. You will be able to see, so clearly, that it is a "them thing" and not a "you thing."

I have had a lot of relationships and love affairs and I do not look back on any of them with regret. I don't wish I had "done things differently." I am absolutely satisfied with them because I know that MY behavior was as good as it could possibly have been. I was doing my best with what I knew (even though sometimes I didn't know much!).

I'm definitely not perfect. But I love a lot, I never quit early, and I nurture my partner's potential. I hope these are qualities I never lose.

If you can continue to do and give your best to your partner, you can rest easy knowing that you did everything you could. That is real integrity, and it's something to be proud of.

ARE YOU A DRAMA ADDICT?

Over the years I've had to work on reprogramming what I am attracted to. If you're a woman who likes to date men, it is important to note that your father's behavior in childhood was imprinted upon your young mind as being "normal." My father was the very definition of inconsistent, and that has led me down the path of being attracted to passionate, excitable men... Who also bring the *drama*.

This has also meant that when I date someone who is not that same type, sometimes I think their lack of frenetic behavior makes them boring. No honey! A partner who has it together is awesome! A partner who is calm and considered is wonderful. A partner whose moods you do not have to tip-toe around is such a blessing.

If this is sounding resonant, don't despair! Just like I have, you can literally change what you are attracted to by reprogramming your brain through tapping. Hypnosis is marvelous too!

LOVE FROM A DISTANCE

This brings me to my next point, which is that sometimes it is healthier for us to love people from a distance, not up-close.

I'm sure you know many people like this: people who are lovely, kind, wonderful... but who have issues that you are simply not interested in navigating. No one is perfect, and everyone has their bouquet of balderdash, but some bouquets just smell too rotten!

This is the delicate dance. We can love unconditionally, but we need to be SELECTIVE about who we do this with! And sometimes, loving unconditionally is something we need to do from a *distance*.

I've had relationships with incredible men who I have also decided are better with a bit of space between us. We are wonderful friends, and it doesn't need to be anything more than that!

I once had this flirtation with a guy who looked like a mix between Ethan Hawke and Matt Dillon in the early 90s. (Yes, delicious.) He was tall, British, funny, and very smart. One day, on the phone, he told me, "You know, I think the problem a lot of people have is that they get along with someone, and they think that just because they get along, they should date or have sex. But that's foolish! Often, you'd just be better as friends."

He is absolutely right! Even if someone is devilishly attractive and has a lot of qualities you admire, you have to ask yourself, 'What would a relationship with this person be like?' When you're getting involved with someone, do some projections of the future! Look at this person, their life, their habits, their goals. What would it really be like if you two lived together, or were committed to one another?

Are they happy with their own company? Does their life have meaning and purpose? Are they interested in being their best self? How is their relationship with their family? What are their friends like? Do they have substance abuse problems?

If the answers to these questions make you feel uneasy, maybe it is best for you to demote that person. I'm sure whoever we are talking about is not a bad person, but you are only interested in the exceptional now. They don't need to share your bed every night for the two of you to enjoy one another's company. A lot of pain could be prevented that way.

UNCONDITIONAL LOVE

So let's say you've done the hard work of appraising another human and you've decided, 'Yes, I'm in! I'm all in! I'm excited about this!'

I believe that in a relationship, unconditional love is the *goal*. Please note that I said goal! And the reason I said goal is because this is something we work towards over time. It may not be there every day. But it is definitely something beautiful and worth striving for.

How do we define this?

Unconditional love is pure, unabiding acceptance of who someone is and where they are at. When we love unconditionally, we don't try to change, fix or manipulate. We don't pout when we don't get our way. Instead, we are truly *free agents.* The deal you make is as follows: the object of your affection is free to do whatever they please, and you don't take it personally.

Unconditional love means that you truly accept whoever you're with in the place that they are in. You don't withhold your love until they do this or resolve that. You are committed to being right here with them in this moment, and you love them fully.

This is a simple concept, yes, but the execution of simple concepts isn't always easy. You will have times in your relationship that you really struggle with this!

The truth is that people are always free to do what they please, but we hold one another to these contracts that, in many ways, limit the scope of acceptability. Eventually, either the contract will be broken, or the relationship will dissolve.

Most love is transactional: "I will love you as long as you behave the way that I want you to, and if you do something I don't like, I will take my love away." But unconditional love says that you respect where they are, and what they're going through.

(Note: this is not to say that you should willingly remain in a situation that is causing you pain. No matter what someone else is doing, and even if we are legally bound to one another, it is still our responsibility to extricate ourselves from harm's way. It is up to us to create a boundary, and then insist upon it.)

And—as I said above—if things are not going so well, we can love unconditionally from a distance!

"We really like it when there's a stubborn person in your life who will not behave the way you need them to in order for you to feel good. Because only a person like that will free you from the madness of trying to get other people to change their ways so that you can feel better. Because it fosters a weakness in you. Everybody's running around, looking for the perfect person who does not even exist. When what you're really wanting is just someone nice that you can play off of while you maintain your vibrational frequency, and then attract, from wherever you are, all that you want.

We think the relationship vows should go something like 'I like you pretty good, let's see how it goes.' Rather than that, 'I promise that

I'll be good to you no matter how rotten you are until we die'? 'I like you pretty good, let's see how it goes. It is my promise to you that I will do my best to look for the positive aspects in you and everyone else. And I hold you not responsible in any way, shape, or form for the way I feel. I am completely responsible for how I'm feeling.'

Now, depending on how well you know them, 'Because I have an inner being, who has a very high opinion of a lot of things, and is transmitting a signal 24 hours a day. And offering that signal. And it is my desire that I be a vibrational match to that, so I cannot focus upon the flaws in you. Because that would put me in a very low signal, and then I couldn't be in vibrational alignment with who I really am. And when I'm not in vibrational alignment with who I really am, then my point of attraction is not what I want it to be, and I don't get what I want from you or from anyone else. So I'm not gonna do that.'"—Abraham-Hicks

THE WAY YOU'RE FEELING INFORMS YOUR FUTURE

Is he my boyfriend? Is she going to be my wife? Are they my babe for life? Oh, so many questions!

Sometimes when it comes to relationships, we give our power away by wanting the other person to define it, to tell us "what it is." Why is it that we give up our power in this way? Why are we always looking to the other person to tell us if it's good or not?

Don't forget: you are an authority in this relationship! (Especially because you understand the power of your mind and the immense sway you have over creating your own world.) So actually, you get to dictate the terms too!

Let's say there's no label on the relationship yet, and sometimes you feel anxiety about that. You kind of want to "lock it down" so that you will feel some sense of security. (Spoiler alert: there is no such thing as security from an external source. Security is something you feel. Period.)

The best thing that you can do, when you fall for someone, is allow *how you feel when you're together* to guide it. Let the way that you feel in their presence inform you. Do you feel seen? Cared for? Loved? When you look in their eyes, what do you perceive? Passion, curiosity, joy, connection? Pay attention to the little things: the questions they ask, the rapidness of their breath, whether they are tense or at ease, how quickly they smile and laugh around you.

Do they tell you they love you, or do they make a practice of actually demonstrating it? How do they speak about you when you're not around? Do they make space and time in their life for you? Does their vision of the future include you?

You might be desperate to know where your relationship is going. But you don't need to consult a psychic or pull tarot cards to know, even though that can be a fun way to access your own guidance. *Your relationship is going wherever you think about.* If you keep focusing on having fun, and what feels good, and all of the delightful and satisfying things, you will get more of them! The positive momentum will simply keep building and the relationship will glow up.

I know that sometimes ideas like this can seem too metaphysical, but they are absolutely grounded in reality. The way that you feel dictates your actions. And your actions create outcomes! This is why I always say that feeling good is your job: because it creates real, tangible *results*.

THE MORE YOU PLEASE OTHERS, THE FASTER IT SHAKES APART

Your job is not simply to feel good. It is also to focus on *pleasing yourself.*

This is one of the reasons why it is so essential to be with someone who really accepts you for who you are. Being with someone who is critical—even if they aren't aware of it—is very dangerous.

Why? Because you want the relationship to work so much that you will start to adapt yourself, ever so slightly, to please them.

And ironically, if you contort and bend over backwards to please them... You will no longer be the person they fell in love with. They won't respect you. The relationship will be over.

For years, I sweated, toiled, and troubled myself over a man. In the beginning, things were amazing. But as he got further from his compass and started to criticize me, I tried to be someone else to make him happy. As I did this, I got further and further from my own compass! Now, neither of us were happy! We were no longer a vibrational match. It shook apart.

It was the first time I had tried to change to please someone else, and it caused me so much pain. If you've ever been in a situation like this, you know precisely how much anguish it puts you through. You start to doubt yourself, your talents, your shine. You start to dull it down. You don't want to be too big because it will only invite more criticism. It is like a slow death.

You cannot "please" someone else. It is their job to please themselves! Redirect your focus to yourself.

KNOW YOUR OUTCOME

It's amazing how many people get into relationships without really knowing what they want... And stay in them without knowing what their partner wants either!

You have to ask yourself, 'What do I want from my relationship?'

This is a very important question and it is one we need to spend some time with. Do you want to be committed to one person? Do you want the freedom to pursue others? Do you want to get married, or does that not matter? Do you want to have children, or would you be happy without them?

Because the reality is that if you want certain things and your partner does not, it is going to create conflict. It is essential that the two of you are on the same page. While you could cajole and manipulate and scam your way into them agreeing with you, it will never last.

Know what it is that you want and then find out what your partner wants. When the two of you are aligned on this, when you share a vision and you are both excited about it, you will be astounded at the speed with which your dream life manifests. Things will spring into being in a way that you could never have conceived. When you are intent on feeling good, allow that to be your dominant goal, and let yourself be led by little impulses... You will be amazed at the way your life begins to take shape.

LEARN TO ENJOY WHERE YOU ARE RIGHT NOW

Recently I have stopped saying the phrase, "I can't wait!" Even though it is a statement of excitement and anticipation, it also indicates a teeny-tiny moment of dissatisfaction with the moment I am in. It's just the slightest energetic wobble, and I'm not here for it! Particularly because *every moment can be delicious* if we choose to see it that way!

If you are in the early days of a relationship, you might be tempted to jump ahead. Maybe you are *dying* for the moment where you take tropical vacations together! Or you move in together, or they start buying you fabulous jewelry! Or whatever other milestone lights up your heart.

That's okay, and I totally understand. Love is so exciting, and it should be! I would simply encourage you to slow down, breathe, and love where you are right now.

There may be so many things you want to create with this person, but each one is an individual step. It's not just about the "big picture," because we are living right now and we want to create in these moments too!

I remember a vision I had of driving around with someone I loved, listening to a particular song as we sang along to it. A couple of weeks later, that's exactly what we were doing. It felt even better than I had imagined it would, and I closed my eyes as he sped down the street, feeling the true ecstasy of being in a moment I had created with my mind... And made manifest!

It was a simple little thing, yes. But the fact of the matter is that *I created it with my mind* and it felt so, so good!

It is so much fun to practice your manifesting skills—which are also your skills of *focus*—in the realm of relationships! You are literally creating your own world, and then inviting someone else to take part in the dance with you.

Allow yourself to daydream about some experiences you would like to share: places you would like to go, moments you would relish, conversations you would love to have, interactions that would thrill you. Close your eyes and let yourself feel them. Allow the joy and excitement to flood your body! These things will come to you... And the better you feel on a daily basis, the faster they will appear.

Relationships will bring us pain so long as we are in a rush to move from one stage to another. If you've ever met (or been!) someone who is in a perfectly good relationship but is desperate to get engaged, you have witnessed firsthand this particular kind of anguish.

It is painful because the person in question simply cannot relax into the moment. To enjoy the unfolding. To let the process of getting to know each other be exactly that—a process. Instead, they are obsessed about getting a ring on their finger, because they think it will bring them some kind of certainty and security. (Surprise! When you get the ring, you are opening yourself to a whole new era of uncertainty and insecurity. IT NEVER ENDS.)

When we are quick to jump into relationships, to put labels on it, to claim someone as "ours," we are depriving ourselves of so much joy. These things take time. In order to see without illusion, we must approach it one day at a time. The act of truly falling in love is a slow-dive. Anything else is just lust or limerence.

Instead of constantly projecting into the distance—a thrilling act which unfortunately throws us out of the moment, also known as "future-tripping"—we can completely calm down our nervous system when we make a commitment to simply BEING HERE NOW.

Make an effort to turn your anxiety into appreciation. When you start dating someone you really like, the urge to future-trip can feel off the charts. Instead, decide that being in the moment will a) be better for your sanity and b) bode well for your actual relationship. Just keep bringing yourself back to the moment with gratitude and mindfulness. Whenever you find yourself thinking, 'I wonder when I will see them again?!', change the conversation in your mind: 'I am so thankful we had such a fun date. I loved getting those texts from them last night. If I never saw them again or I got hit by a bus tomorrow, I would be totally satisfied with what had already occurred!'

Sometimes this will be challenging, but the further you can sink into appreciation and gratitude, the better off you will be. I promise.

AS LONG AS YOUR SECURITY IS DEPENDENT ON ANOTHER, YOU'RE INSECURE

If the only way you can feel good about your life is when your partner—or potential partner—does something that pleases you, you are in for a rocky road. And not the kind full of marshmallows!

We all struggle with this! We ride the rollercoaster: "They texted me! WHEE! We haven't seen each other in a few days. BOOOOO!" It feels great and then it feels uncertain! We go up and then we go down! What a world.

It would probably be mildly sociopathic to not have your emotional needle at all moved by what your partner is doing—or not doing! So don't beat yourself up too much if you don't nail this every single time. But the ideal is to be *consistent* in your own emotions as much as possible.

The best thing that we can do, then, in situations like this, is to build such a strong life for ourselves that our partner is not our only source of joy. Throw yourself into whatever else it is that you love—your work, the gym, macrame, cooking, reading, school, travel, saving your money—and create a life that is robust and delicious.

This way, your lover is just frosting on top of the gateaux that is your life! 'Cause expecting them to show up with the batter, mix it, pour it, bake it, and then decorate it... is a lot. And I can almost guarantee that if this is the vibe you're bringing to relationships—even if it's just a WHIFF—your potential love will run for the hills.

Get high on your own supply, babe. You can literally never go wrong with this!

DON'T TAKE ANYTHING PERSONALLY

One of my favorite books is *The Four Agreements*, written by impeccable Virgo Don Miguel Ruiz. The book presents four guidelines for living well, and the second one is simple: don't take anything personally.

This idea, when you truly implement it in your life, is actually earth-shattering. It changes everything.

Imagine how chill your life would be if you didn't take *anything* that other people did personally. If you were able to brush off any insult, unanswered text message, facial expression, or rude behavior quickly and easily, because you knew—categorically—that it was *not about you?*

We can walk around this world taking offense to everything that everyone does. It's an option, for sure! But it leaves us powerless. It's like being inside a pinball machine, where everyone else's behavior is operating the flippers. You're simply at their mercy. You are reacting. You are a pawn!

But if you can realize that other people's behavior has nothing to do with you, you can feel peace. You can take back control. You can own yourself, your energy, your moods.

Think about the last time you were rude to someone, or lacking in compassion, or impatient. Was it really about them? No, of course it wasn't! You might have been mad at them in the moment, but really, your ire was directed at them because of something else that was going on. People who are happy and content simply do not treat others badly!

It can be hard to remember this when you get poor service or someone decides to deposit some trifling nonsense on your doorstep. But the truth is that you *never* know what someone is really going through. Maybe your impatient Uber driver is in the middle of a divorce. Maybe your boss is in a bad mood because her mom is sick and she's worried beyond belief. Maybe your lover is struggling with something they don't feel ready to tell you about yet.

We need to start to make a practice of giving people the benefit of the doubt. People always—always!—have a reason for behaving the way that they do. If you chose to give people some leeway and to sink into the knowledge that it is not about you, how would this change your life?

Learning to think this way is a matter of discipline and practice. Humans habitually choose thoughts that are painful, sad, or otherwise harmful, simply because we are used to them. They are part of our routine! To get scientific about it, these are well-worn neural pathways that our mind is accustomed to taking. They're like eight-lane freeways, whereas the neural pathway labeled "Maybe they had a good reason for what they did" is more like a gravel road. It takes work, effort, and practice to turn your car (aka your mind) onto this gravel road and traverse it, whereas the eight-lane freeway is like cruising down easy street.

It will take some practice, for sure. But it is truly worth it. It will lead you to freedom and the ability to feel good, no matter what is going on around you.

NOBODY ELSE IS RESPONSIBLE FOR YOUR HAPPINESS

Sometimes in relationships we give our power away by believing that it is the other person's job to make us happy. Pay attention for one second: this is completely untrue, and believing it will only bring you pain!

No one else can make you happy! It is something you must own for yourself. This is a non-negotiable!

Yes, in the beginning, you might think, 'This person is making me happy!' Getting cute text messages and anticipating the next date feels fantastic. But soon the thrill of that will fade, at least a little bit... And you will essentially be back to square one. If, in that state, you are constantly looking to your partner to give you a rush, you are setting yourself up for disaster.

Two unhappy people who are always looking to each other to try to feel some joy is a recipe for misery. However, two happy people who are operating independently of one anothers' moods will always work!

This is why I constantly stress the importance of feeling good. When you can come to your relationship already feeling good, you have so much to give! But if you are stressed out, anxious, and focused on your misery, you will bring that energy to the relationship and it will feel terrible.

If your work, friends and interests light you up, you have so much more to bring home to your partner. When *life itself* is filling your cup, it's easy to pour the overflow into your beloved. But when life is stressing you out, when all you choose to notice are the negative things, you'll come home and be destructive.

I remember being in an open relationship. It was short-lived, but it taught me some fascinating things. One of the things that really surprised me was the way that my *other* partner could add to my primary relationship. I found that after spending the evening with her, I had so much *more* love and affection to give to my boyfriend. I was already happy, and when I was with her, she showed me such deep affection and sweetness. All those emotions filled my cup, which I was then able to pass along.

By the time I would go home to my man, I felt transformed by her kindness and gentleness. It opened my heart up in such a beautiful way.

That was such a surprising side-effect of being in an open relationship, and one that I would never have been able to predict. But it is a very visceral demonstration of how, when we already feel good, we have so much more to give. It also shows the way that when we feel good, we attract *more of the same.*

We are all in charge of how we feel, no matter what is going on in our lives. Even if you are really struggling with something right now, your mind is the one thing that you can control! Learning to think better thoughts is a practice, and it gets easier the more that you do it. Make your mind work for you... Not against you.

TUNE YOURSELF TO THE BEST PART OF YOUR PARTNER

If you're currently in a relationship, close your eyes and conjure up a vision of your beloved in your head. First, think of all the things they do that annoy you! Ooooh! How enraging!

Now, wipe the slate clean and think of all the reasons why you love them and the ways they make your life better.

I ask you: which one felt better?

Obviously, thinking about the reasons why you like them is going to feel better.

When you're in a relationship—and you want to stay in it!—focusing on the best parts of your partner is always the move. ALWAYS. No one is perfect, and your partner certainly isn't, but are you going to let your focus on that ruin your relationship?

Now, this is not to say that you should turn a blind eye when your partner is doing something that is deliberately harmful, manipulative, or otherwise shady. I would never advocate staying in a relationship where you are not respected. But if your relationship is positive, and you are enjoying it, do yourself a favor and think about why you like your partner as much as possible!

On a metaphysical level, trying to "fix problems" rarely, if ever, works. The reason for this is that whatever you put your focus on will grow and expand! If you keep thinking about what is wrong, obsessing over the lack of this or that, you will create more of the same. But it is possible to overcome problems by thinking of them differently! By seeing them as an opportunity for growth and greater intimacy. By thinking about how you want it to be, and deploying whatever tools you have.

Abraham-Hicks talks a lot about "focusing on the wrong end of the stick." For example, with every subject there are two ways we can look at it. We can look at having the thing, how good that feels, the excitement around it. Or we can look at the absence of it, obsess over its lack in our life, and get all pent up about it.

The same is true in a relationship. We can fixate on the problems, on what they're not doing, on how it isn't the way we'd like it... Or we can see opportunities, deeply respect and value our partner, and be grateful.

I suggest the latter!

GET MORE EXCITED ABOUT FEELING GOOD THAN ABOUT YOUR RELATIONSHIP!

Just as our partner is not responsible for our happiness, it is essential that we do not depend on our relationships to be happy.

Relationships come and go, but your life is your life forever! Make enjoying your time on the planet your primary goal, rather than viewing your life as an intermittent gasp between what your partner wants or needs.

Here are some ways that I amp up my life so that I am not just sitting around wondering about some love interest...

I learn new skills ❤ do breathwork ❤ go to comedy shows ❤ daydream ❤ work out ❤ go to dance classes ❤ take photographs ❤ go on long exploratory walks ❤ perform rituals ❤ create new projects that challenge me ❤ travel with my best friends ❤ attend workshops ❤ get dressed up just because it feels good ❤ tap ❤ go to art shows ❤ find new ways to be of service ❤ listen to lectures and audiobooks and make notes ❤ take long baths ❤ decorate my home ❤ visualize what I desire ❤ say yes to exciting invitations ❤ dance and sing all over my house ❤ go on adventures ❤ talk on the phone for hours... just to name a few!

All of these things infuse my life with joy, purpose, and excitement.

When you double-down on your own life, romantic fluctuations are less distracting. And if you've ever been in a relationship where you essentially gave up your own life to be in a partnership, you know how hard it is when it ends... Because you don't even remember who you are or what you love!

Be in the driver's seat of your own life. It makes everything else so much sweeter. ✳

"If you raise your standards but don't really believe you can meet them, you've already sabotaged yourself. You won't even try; you'll be lacking the sense of certainty that allows you to tap the deepest capacity that's within you. Our beliefs are like unquestioned commands, telling us how things are, what's possible and impossible and what we can and cannot do. They shape every action, every thought and every feeling that we experience. As a result, changing our belief systems is central to making any real and lasting change in our lives." —Tony Robbins

09

CHANGE YOUR MIND, CHANGE YOUR LIFE

Y OU MAY HAVE BEEN SURPRISED THAT THE LAST TWO chapters—about manifesting the love of your life—were more about raising your standards than anything else. That's because I believe that love is easy! The world is overflowing with wonderful people who think you are the best thing since sliced bread!

You can find love anywhere. It is not hard to come by. There are not a limited number of soulmates in the world: they're everywhere! So the chapter about love was actually about being choosy, because if you can have *anything*, why not have the best?

I'd love for us all to be extremely choosy about everything in our lives. Where we live, what we do for a living, how we spend our free time, what we eat, and how we dress. Wouldn't it be wonderful to raise our standards in every aspect of our lives?

The truth is that our standards go hand-in-hand with whether we can hold on to the things we have manifested. Because as humans, we have a nasty little habit. A habit of self-sabotage. A habit of going backwards once we've gotten what we think we want. And it's all about our beliefs: what we believe is appropriate, and what we're worthy of.

Imagine, for a second, that after a couple of months of practicing feeling good, you are approached in a restaurant by a stranger. This stranger is very attractive, charismatic, kind, intelligent, and successful. They strike up a conversation with you, ask you on a date, and pretty quickly, the two of you are seeing each other all the time.

It is everything you have ever dreamed of. You are so excited about it.

But soon, you find yourself getting insecure. Saying things that you know will drive a wedge between you. Flirting with someone else. It all falls apart.

Here's another scenario. Imagine, if you will, that you've had a whopping financial year. Your bank account is bulging. You've never seen so much money in there before! You are delighted, and you feel so good.

So you start spending. You buy yourself a hot car, a bunch of rare art, you hire an interior decorator and completely redo your house. Or maybe you hire a live-in chef and book three international cruises. Or you join a Caviar Of The Month

Club. (Oh, I don't know! Pick your poison!) Before long, your bank account is no longer bulging. In fact, you have to start watching your ass!

As I have told you over and over again, manifesting is easy. People do it all the time without even knowing that this is what they're doing! But holding on to the things that we have manifested? That is a different story!

Why is this? Why, after finally obtaining something that we want so badly, does it sometimes start to head south?

This chapter is about how we can prevent self-sabotage once we get something we want. This relates to love and relationships just as much as it relates to anything else: a great career, a healthy body, and the list goes on.

There is nothing in life that is one-and-done, where you tick an achievement off the list and you get to ignore it afterwards. Anything you want that is worthwhile or valuable to you will be something that you will need to continue working at, putting energy toward, and constantly improving upon. If your relationship isn't getting better, it is getting worse... And the same is true of your business, your fitness, and all the rest of it.

We don't do what we are capable of. *We simply live our beliefs!*

Our behavior is influenced by our beliefs, our standards, and our stories.

This is where it all loops back around. This is where it ties back to radical self-love, which is really the practice of raising our opinion of ourselves. This is where we have to work on our worthiness, on the belief that we deserve good things. And it is where we get clear about what we will and will not tolerate or accept, both from others and from ourselves.

All of our progress actually comes from breaking habits that no longer serve us.

WHY DO WE SELF-SABOTAGE?

I'm sure you know someone—maybe even you!—who has had this experience. Things are going well, and you do something to screw it up. Maybe you don't follow up after an important meeting. Maybe you tell yourself, "It'll never work anyway." Maybe you procrastinate like mad. And maybe you start saying, out loud, things that you *know* the other party won't enjoy hearing!

One of the reasons for self-sabotage is that our standards won't allow us to experience more—or less—than we think we deserve.

For example, if you feel comfortable with $10,000 in your bank account, and you make a deposit that puts your balance at $19,000, you will usually spend the "extra" $9000 so you're back to where you feel safe. But if you only have $8000 in there, you'll do whatever it takes to gain the extra $2000.

We all operate like this when it comes to money. You may have not even noticed it, but ask yourself, where does your bank balance ordinarily sit?

That tells you what your money standards are! It's wild, too, because for as many people who are comfortable at $10,000, there are just as many who are comfortable at $100,000. Or $1,000,000! It is all a matter of our *standards*, which are tied into our beliefs.

You may have noticed this in your romantic life, too. If your standards are low, then going out with someone who wants to spoil you and lavish you with gifts may actually feel uncomfortable and a bit weird! Sure, on the surface it looks great, and maybe you are even excited when they show up with flowers or throw a loose diamond or two in your dinner napkin! But if you don't really think you deserve it, your subconscious will throw a fit. This could easily lead to self-sabotage.

Your standards are your beliefs, simply put into action. So if you believe, "I am lazy," your standards are where you put that into practice. Your standards are where the rubber meets the road.

Where does this all come from? Do they just appear out of thin air? Do we decide them in childhood? Well, both! Our beliefs and values are either modeled or something we've chosen to *rebel against.* In other words, we either adopt the same beliefs and values as the people we grew up with, or we do the opposite.

People who have come from very difficult beginnings and transformed themselves into super-over-achievers are often *rebelling* against what they saw and were told at a young age. And then you've certainly heard of people from wealthy, successful families who throw it all away. Again, those people are rebelling against what they experienced in their formative years!

So we have these beliefs which control our lives, most of which we have been dragging around since childhood. If you believe that men can't be trusted, that you will never have a lot of money, that asking for what you want will only result in rejection, then of course your life is going to be small, full of pain, and really confusing! Of course these beliefs are going to dictate your behavior.

The problem with our beliefs is that we often forget to trace things back and really look at them. We find ourselves acting in a way that is incongruous with what we want, and we think, 'Why am I doing this?! I don't want this!' Have you ever had this experience? It's because you are acting upon your subconscious beliefs! For most people, these beliefs—which are essentially the roadmap for our lives—remain unexamined.

The other thing that controls us is our very human desire to move towards pleasure and away from pain. We want everything that feels good and nothing that feels bad!

But let's get clear about the stuff that "feels bad." Anything that feels bad does so because it brings up pain. All pain is fear. Fear of failure, fear of success, fear of rejection, fear of the unknown, fear of what other people think, and the list goes on. These fears run our lives.

The problem comes when something that we want will require us to experience some pain in order to get it. Because everything that you can think of—a person, a subject, or an idea—comes with its own neuro-associations. A neuro-association is an emotional link to a subject.

Let's take the subject of working out. For almost everyone, this subject comes with neuro-associations of both pain and pleasure.

Imagine, if you will, a young man named Charles. When Charles thinks about exercising, the pain link tells him that working out is tiring, it's hard, he doesn't want to do it, he doesn't know how to do it, and it'll never make a difference anyway. And his pleasure link tells him that going to the gym is good for him... But that's about it.

Look at how much power the pain link has versus the pleasure link! When he thinks of working out, it is a painful subject. He doesn't want to go through all that! Even though he knows that "working out is good for him," there is too much resistance there. He has too many pain links. He'll never go to the gym!

Whichever neuro-association is stronger and more powerful—pleasure or pain—will win.

Let's take this same subject, and we'll use me as an example, because I am someone who has re-wired my *neuro-associations* around working out and exercise.

When I first started working out with a personal trainer, I told myself the most disempowering stories! I would resist every exercise. In my head, I'd say, "I'm so tired! I can't do it anymore! I need a break!" I'd look in the mirror while doing squats and critique my body.

But after a little while, I decided that wasn't working. So I started to tell myself new stories.

These days, when I think about working out, I think: YES! This is something I enjoy! I love getting out of my house in a cute outfit and working towards the body of my dreams. I really enjoying spending time with my trainer, he pushes me hard and we laugh the whole time. And many years ago, I started I telling myself that my body responds quickly to exercise, and—shock horror—it does! I love the results from working out.

In fact, I have re-wired my neuro-associations so much that it has *changed my beliefs* about who I am as a person. When it's time for me to go to the gym, I don't hem and haw, I don't procrastinate, I don't think of excuses. I get dressed and I go! I am actually—could you believe it—excited to go! There is no negotiation, there is no hesitation. I work out 5-6 days a week because I believe I am fit, I believe I am someone who has a great body, I believe I am someone who takes care of themselves. I don't skip workouts because I believe I am consistent. And I enjoy going because *I believe I can see an improvement every single time I go.*

As much as we all love to feel good, there may be some areas or subjects in your life where it may seem almost impossible to feel good because your neuro-associations are so negative. When it comes to a situation like that, it is imperative that we re-wire so that we can start to feel good about things that used to make us feel bad!

There are many ways to re-wire, including tapping (my favorite), hypnosis, NLP (Neuro-Linguistic Programming) and the list goes on.

Hypnosis is one of my favorite secret weapons, and I'm deeply blessed to have a close friend, Grace Smith, who is one of the best hypnotherapists on the planet. We have worked together on many different subjects, like levels of abundance, letting go of emotional guardedness, and healing past relationships. Hypnosis is super-cool because it's like getting into your subconscious mind through the back door. It's relaxing and really effective!

There are so many great techniques that I encourage you to try. Tapping has always been my favorite, because I can do it whenever I want, in a short amount of time, and for free.

I believe that you should use the technique that works best for you, and that might not be tapping. But what I will say is that ideally, this technique should be something you can use at the drop of a hat. We don't always love doing the work of rewiring ourselves, so the fewer barriers between you and the solution, the better!

Look, as long as every time you think about a subject you feel pain, *it will be impossible for you to feel good.* If you want to manifest a beautiful relationship, but every time you think about commitment you are flooded with pain and fear, you will literally keep what you want at an energetic arm's length.

This is why it is absolutely essential that we change our conditioned responses to the subjects that we have tension or resistance around. If you've been digging into the Book Bonuses, you've been working through your resistance this whole time! You have been breaking old neuro-associations and creating new ones. You have been dismantling old beliefs and stories, and replacing them with new ones that light you up. Isn't that incredible? So now you know—beyond a shadow of a doubt—that your neuro-associations can be broken, and easily!

When we are able to think of a previously contentious topic and feel good about it, the entire game is changed!

Do you know how easy it is to focus on feeling good when you have *no conflict in your mind?* It's a cakewalk! I used to find it so difficult to think new thoughts and focus on feeling good because practically every subject that popped into my mind had a negative link. It reminded me of pain or my ineptitude or how far I still had to go. With tapping, we can completely change our neuro-associations. What would it feel like to think about, say, your relationship with your father and have no *emotional drag*, no conflict, no tension?! And just imagine how that would improve the time you spent together!

I love the fact that we can heal ourselves by using our own bodies. With tapping, we can literally rewire ourselves so that ANY SUBJECT is conflict-free. How much peace and freedom would you have if there was no resentment or heaviness around anything?! Well, how much peace and freedom can you handle?! This is why tapping was originally called EFT: Emotional Freedom Technique. When you are emotionally free, anything is possible. Everything is possible!

Imagine a woman who is starting a business but is terrified that it won't work. Every morning, she wakes up and is filled with dread. She wants it to be a success but she is emanating fear every single day. What would you estimate her results to be? How long until she shutters for good?

The quality of the results in our life are due to our actions, and it is our *beliefs* that drive our actions. They are always the cause of our behavior! So would this theoretical woman be engaging in actions that were brave, risky, bold, and decisive? Probably not! She would probably be hedging her bets, avoiding anything too challenging, because she feels like she is only ever just treading water.

Now, take this same woman and remove her fear. Remove her neuro-associations that tell her that risks cause pain, businesses cause trouble, and that she's not good enough.

If she did this, even if she had the same businesses in the same premises, she would behave completely differently. Even if she didn't have any positive neuro-associations and she just had NEUTRAL ones instead of negative ones, her business would be transformed! When you have no resistance, you can dream HUGE! Take big risks! Ask for help! And expand your life beyond what you ever thought possible.

The real magic in our lives is in transforming how we feel about things. How we see things. I have said this for years: magic is a shift in perception. Because those shifts empower and embolden us to do things *differently*. And thus, we change the entire direction of our lives.

I encourage you to take a close look at the areas of your life where you are not experiencing the results that you'd really like to see. Ask yourself, 'When I think about X, what comes up for me?' Get really quiet and listen. Do some free-associating on a piece of paper and be curious about what arises. If you notice that you have a bunch of negative neuro-associations to the things that are important to you, get serious and *tap it out!* ✳

10

HOW TO BE A HIGH VIBE HONEY

STARTED WRITING ABOUT RADICAL SELF-LOVE BACK IN 2011, after having made it the priority in my life in 2006. When I decided that loving myself was the most important thing I could do with my time and my energy, my entire life transformed. I released the clinical depression and eating disorder I had been living with for such a long time. I moved to Australia, and then to New York. I started my own business with the intention of helping other women make similar transitions.

The reason I am so passionate about what I do is because I have been on the other side, and I see all that pain, worry and anxiety as a massive barrier to the life that you actually want. If your desires for your life include creativity, juicy abundance, thriving relationships and vibrant health, feeling stuck, lost, small or uncertain is only going to hold you back.

When my first book came out in 2016, my greatest vision for it was that women who read it would change the way they treated themselves, and then their daughters, through observing that, would grow up to be happier and healthier. A noble goal, sure. But now... I have a bigger, brighter vision.

The journey from self-loathing to self-love is an important one, and one that I believe in wholeheartedly. It is an important thing to do. It creates a healthy, stable foundation upon which you can build.

But I don't want us to stop there! I want us to go STRATOSPHERIC. I don't just want you to think you're a good person. I want you to acknowledge that you are all-powerful, a juicy goddess who lives a charmed life! A bad bitch writ large, who doesn't solicit other people's opinions before she makes a move!

Why shouldn't you live as the embodiment of the goddess you are? Let's go big. Let's go hard. I love it!

And it gets better.

I have realized that if I want *you* to succeed in a major way, then I have to lead by example. If I want you to ask for more from your life, I have to demand more from myself and then show you how I did it! If I want you to own your choices and be bold, I have to be *even more bold* in my own.

It is up to me to set enormous goals that make me gulp. It is up to me to declare what I am going to do, and then *go out* and *do it*. It is up to me to put my foot down and say *no thank you* when an offer is not good enough. It is up to me to guard my energy and not squander it on people, places, and situations that are not furthering my cause. It is up to me to cut out any activities that are draining my vibe or optimism. It is up to me to be the BAD BITCH of my own life.

Truth be told, this realization—although big!—is one of the most fun realizations of my lifetime! Once I truly came to grips with the fact that the bigger I am, the bigger it will encourage those around me to go, it became blatantly clear that I could no longer make excuses.

When the idea of bettering yourself isn't just about you alone, but about uplifting the community you belong to, everything changes.

This doesn't just apply to me, it applies to you too. You may think that no one notices you, but that's not true. You are influencing your entire community every single day. So if you want your influence to be a positive one—if you want the people around you to love themselves, have faith, take risks and live their most fabulous lives—you have to lead by example!

When it's just about you, it's easy to run out of steam. It's easier to make excuses because who cares if you slip up today? No one will notice.

But if the idea is that when you excel, everyone else excels along with you... Your whole existence shifts. When you realize that your lack of commitment, your fear, and your low standards will affect other people, your tune changes quickly!

"Self-improvement" can sometimes seem like a burden, but when it's framed up in this new way, it takes a different shape. The improvement of the self becomes the improvement of everyone, and what a privilege and an honor to have that as your life's mission!

Burden? No, honey. How is it a burden to have more fun than ever? How is it a burden to expect more from your life? How is it a burden to enjoy yourself more, level up, surprise and delight yourself by continually pushing forward?!

So let's talk about what it requires to play at this level in our lives. Is it as simple as making a decision and putting our best Balenciaga boot forward?

Not entirely, although of course, making the decision and committing to it is a major key.

The quality of our lives, and the level at which we are able to play, is inextricably linked to the quality and level of our ENERGY.

When you are energized, you can do anything. When you are exhausted, you just want to stay in bed. So how do we make our energy work for us?

I have vivid memories of sitting in the audience at a Tony Robbins event. Okay, "sitting" is the wrong word. I had a seat, sure, next to my dynamic Aries pal Natalia Benson. But we didn't do a lot of sitting. No, instead, for four days, we jumped up and down, we screamed with glee, and we danced while standing on top of our chairs. It felt phenomenal! The high was unlike *anything else. Nothing* feels better than truly tapping into your own energy and realizing how deep the well runs.

It was my second time at Unleash The Power Within, and whenever I tell people about it, they ask me, "What's the best thing you learned?"

Both times, I learned about energy.

At UPW, Tony is regularly on stage for 12 hours at a time. He is teaching, yelling, dancing, jumping, and air-drumming with two enormous sticks! I think he takes a couple of bathroom breaks, but mostly, he is *going hard*. It is a wonder to witness, and it's not a rarity. He does exactly this, on stages all across the world, all year long!

Tony leads from the front. His energy is so impressive that it inspires everyone in the audience to go just as hard! The best thing I learned from attending one of his events is that as you tap into your own energy source, over and over again, over the course of four days, you realize... *I have so much more to give.*

It's in these moments that you become massively aware that—just like feeling good—having a high level of energy is a choice. And just like feeling good, it is something you can activate! Feeling good rarely just "happens," and being energetic rarely just "happens" either.

We feel good because we have made a choice to do so and we have taken specific actions that will get us there. This is something you have been practicing as you work your way through this book.

You will be delighted to hear that being energetic is the exact same thing: you make a choice to increase your energy and then you do certain things to make it happen!

A lot of people don't want to hear this. They use their lack of energy as an excuse to avoid living the kind of life they really dream about.

"I would do it," they sigh, "But I'm just so tired."

No, mama.

You might be tired... But the secondary benefit of being tired is that it's a fantastic, convenient excuse for not going after what you want! It's an easy way to wriggle out of your fear of failure... And your fear of success! It's a guaranteed method to stay small and safe and not be criticized!

If you peeked underneath your all-consuming tiredness, you might just find a whole lot of fear.

And if, instead of arguing for your limitations, you made the commitment that you were going to increase your energy levels every day no matter what, you would discover that there is absolutely nothing you cannot do.

Elevated energy makes things easy! It feels good to be in that state. And it feels good for other people to be around that, too! Want more friends and romantic involvements? Lift your energetic game! It's like catnip for everyone else. Completely irresistible.

The truth is that when you increase your energy levels you will realize that there is no problem that is too big. You can figure out absolutely everything! No matter what is going on in your life, when you approach it with huge amounts of energy, you'll find that issues, complications and interpersonal riddles don't stand a chance!

Imagine someone who wants to accomplish something in their life. Let's use you, for example! See yourself in your mind's eye, and see the thing that you are working towards beside you. Now, ask yourself, what would happen in this movie if the star—that's you!—had *unlimited amounts of energy?*

You would wake up early and stay up late to get things done. You would do the research—joyfully! You would make the phone calls, ask for help, and find inspiration in the unlikeliest of places. You would make time for yourself, and when you were in those moments of ecstatic relaxation, solutions would unfold... Easily.

God, doesn't that sound so good?! I am high just writing about it!

To go back to my original point, my favorite thing about being in Tony Robbins' presence is that you are reminded of the absolute importance of having massive amounts of *energy*. If he was tired, thinking about how jetlagged he was, or the fact that he's done a million of these events already, how would that impact his audience?

Their energy would plummet! Their attention would waver. There is no way he would be able to hold them in the palm of his hand for four days!

One of my least favorite things is going to an event or a class or even listening to a podcast where the person being featured starts off by talking about how tired or jetlagged they are. Talk about a downer! I want to yawn just listening to it.

Okay, I am not a total tyrant. I get it. We have all had those days, weeks, months, maybe even years where energy appears to be in short supply. Where you simply feel exhausted. Where no matter how much coffee you drink, and no matter how many hours of sleep you get, you are still yawning your face off all day long.

And sometimes this is unavoidable. If you're doing deep healing work, your body will need plenty of time to rest and integrate. If you're in a relationship that feels suffocating, you'll have less energy. It happens.

But we still have the opportunity to fire on all cylinders if we want to.

Energy comes from our body and the actions that we take. The things that we do! Our physiology (body) informs our psychology (mind)! Put simply, if you want to *feel better*, you have to do something physically to create that change. It doesn't just happen in a vacuum.

Jump up and down. Dance. Sing. Do push-ups. Tap. Do a handstand. Laugh!

We manifest more quickly—and we have much deeper reserves of energy—when we consider our bodies when we are making magic.

In this chapter, we are going to explore new ways to raise our energy, because when you have more than enough energy, you can do anything!

USE YOUR BODY

This is the easiest and most practical advice ever: to have more energy, you have to use your body. It is no longer acceptable to consider yourself as mostly a brain which your body just happens to carry around! We are not living from the neck up anymore.

Your body is a battery that charges itself, and the only way it gets charged is by physical activity. If you can walk, do that. If you can dance, do that. We all have different levels of ability so it is up to you to take ownership of what is possible for you. It doesn't matter what it is, just as long as you are doing something—anything!—physical.

When you are feeling tired, think of it as the perfect opportunity to prove otherwise! Sometimes when we feel tired, what our brain is actually telling us is that it's bored. It needs a new challenge!

So why not give yourself a new challenge by choosing to *push through* in those moments when you feel like taking a nap? Prove yourself wrong!

Sometimes it's not that you're exhausted, but your brain needs a reset. One of my favorite tricks when I'm feeling really spent is to line up a guided meditation, lie down, and let my brain relax. By the time the meditation is over, which is usually within 20 or 30 minutes, I feel refreshed and completely ready to tackle whatever is next.

YOU HAVE SO MUCH MORE TO GIVE!

By now, you are well aware of the power of the words that you repeat in your head. As we have worked through this book together, you have started to pay more attention to the things that are echoing in your mind, day in and day out.

Many of these stories have been dismantled with the tapping we've done, and a lot of the others are well on their way to being a distant memory. But now it is time to ask, 'What do I tell myself about my energy level?'

You see, the problem is that many of us are running a constant loop in our mind that goes something like this: 'God, it's early. I'm so tired. I need coffee. I don't wanna do this! I can't be bothered. This is exhausting. Is it time for a nap? I'm so tired. I need some sugar. When will this day be over? I'M SO TIRED!'

When you are feeding yourself with messages like this, it is no wonder you are exhausted! Who wouldn't be?! Our mind believes everything—yes, everything—we put into it! So are you surprised when you're mainlining a story that literally sucks the energy from your bones?

It is time for an energy revolution, and that starts with new messaging. Grab a piece of paper and write, **I have so much more to give!**

Start to make this message an integral part of your internal programming. Tap it in every morning! Imagine if you rewired your brain so that every time you thought you were reaching exhaustion, you remembered that you have so much more to give? How would that change your life?

Seriously: what if this was the thing you told yourself day in and day out? What if you adopted this as your life philosophy, rather than living in a tit-for-tat universe? Make this your daily mantra. Chant it in the morning, make it the wallpaper on your phone, tattoo it on your arm!

"I have so much more to give!" Yes! Yes, you do!

Tell yourself this when you feel exhausted. When you come back from lunch and you want to take a nap; when you're at the gym and don't feel like you can do another rep; when your daughter or partner or parent is trying your damn patience! Remind yourself to dig deep. Remember that you have so much more to give!

This is one of the most powerful messages we can claim. We can either think and reinforce ideas that shut us down, turn us off, use us up... Or we can center our lives around thoughts that are like an IV drip of vitamins!

When you tell yourself that you have so much more to give, you are tapping into an endless well of energy. I'm telling you now: you really do have so much more to give. More than you think!

That's how it goes. The more energy we have, the more it becomes possible. The bigger our vision becomes. And the more excited we are to wake up in the morning and kick ass.

We are either using our minds to help us or to hinder us. It is so important that we learn to use our minds to help us evolve, push through, and get stronger, because when we do this, our lives grow and our possibilities become endless.

WHAT WOULD IT TAKE TO HAVE THE MOST ENERGY IN THE ROOM?

Most of us live in a fairly unconscious way. Even if you are one of the rare few who is aware of, say, the stories you're telling yourself, are you giving much thought—if any—to the way that you walk into a room?

Our lives are absolutely full of fresh starts. It's not just your birthday, or the new year, or every morning. In every single moment, we are granted the divine opportunity to begin again; to start over; to do it differently! Every room you walk into, every conversation you start, every time you get in your car heralds the dawn of something new.

So I love this question, 'What would it take to have the most energy in the room?' because it can help you reframe so many different situations in your life and approach them with a new mindset.

Sometimes when we walk into a new room, we are preoccupied with an avalanche of thoughts that cause anxiety. 'Who is in here? What are they thinking about me? Are they looking at me? What do they want? How can I please them? How do I escape?'

How would it feel if, instead of letting these old, disempowering beliefs run the show, you asked yourself what it would take to have the most energy in the room?

Because, through no fault of your own, someone else in the room may have more power, authority, experience, or skill than you do. But energy has no barrier. No matter your age, race, gender, or ability, you can have more energy than anyone else!

The truth is that most people suffer from a tragic and absolute lack of energy. They drag their cabooses slowly from one place to the next, surviving on caffeine and gossip and not enough vegetables. They grizzle and play small and stare at their phones so much they have a permanent crick in the neck.

But then, here you come! Sauntering into the room like a big delicious minty breath of fresh air! So fresh you could be the Alps, baby! You can floor them with your energy, your enthusiasm, your openness, your hot attitude!

What could you do if you had the most energy in the room? A better question might be, what couldn't you do?!

It's actually easy to do this. It's a walk in the park. A doddle! All it takes is an awareness and a commitment to doing it.

IF YOU'RE TIRED ALL THE TIME...

It is essential to ask yourself why. There could be a few contributing factors— maybe not enough exercise, or eating the wrong kinds of food—but we easily forget about the emotional reasons for being exhausted.

I was in a relationship once that started off so beautifully, but as time wore on, and our misalignment became more apparent, I found myself feeling so *tired* all the time. I wanted to go to bed early and sleep in every day. The basic maintenance that the relationship required felt so taxing that I didn't have any energy for anything else. That tiredness turned into anxiety, which made it harder to get everything else in my life done too!

When our relationship came to an end, I literally felt like a new person. I started jumping out of bed with excitement in the mornings, and I became more productive and creative than ever.

My point is simply that sometimes we are tired because there is something in our lives that is truly draining our energy. It might be a person, a job, or a role that we feel we have to play. Those things can both drain our energy and make us want to sleep all the time, just so we don't have to deal with it!

Of course, if you are chronically exhausted it is important to see a medical professional and make sure you are physically healthy. But if your results come back and they can't find anything, it is essential to look at your environment, the things you're doing, and the people you surround yourself with.

All the energy vampires and leaks have got to go!

USE YOUR ENERGY TO CREATE—AND TEND TO—A VISION

In order to create incredible things in your life, you need to know what you want those things to be!

I remember watching an interview where the owner of a big talent agency talked about how two of his biggest stars first approached the game. They had both walked into his office, sat down with him, and given him a play-by-play of exactly how they saw their careers panning out. No big surprise, then, that this is precisely what happened for them!

Can you imagine that? Can you imagine meeting the absolute top person in your industry, sitting down opposite them, and telling them your vision for how your career was going to go? How much money you were going to make, what glass ceilings you were going to shatter, what you were going to experience, and what you were going to add to the industry as a whole?

I love thinking about this, just as an exercise in expanding your vision and powering up. Close your eyes and envision having a meeting with some gatekeeper, or anyone who keeps watch over the industry that you're in. In your imagination, see yourself telling them—with total confidence and enthusiasm— your big, glorious vision. Tell them exactly what you are going to do and when! Tell them how much money you're going to make! Tell them about what you're going to contribute and how you are going to help people!

Something I've done in the past is write up a list of my ideal future accomplishments, in the format of a press release. I added in any distinctions I had yet to receive, places I wanted to be featured, or clients I wanted to work with. Just like in the Magical Morning Practice, I wrote them in the *past tense...*

And then, in a marvelous stroke of manifestation, when these things actually happen in the real world, I would just copy and paste them onto the About page on my website!

This is how you actively create your future, rather than being a passive passenger.

Nobody knows what the limits of your life, career, or legacy could be. Nobody! So don't leave your future and the fruits of your labor in someone else's hands. Don't believe the gate-keepers who say no, or the so-called industry experts who have no imagination. Asd you've been learning, people are massively limited by their own low self-worth, their lack of faith in the universe, and what they have seen before. Don't let anybody else impose *their* limitations on *you!*

If you have a meeting with someone and they tell you no, or that it won't work, or that you're delusional, know this: you are simply talking to the wrong person. Where there's a will, there's a way!

Boring people have boring visions. Limited people have limited vision. Fearful people have fearful vision. But you don't have to be restricted by *any* of that because you are in charge!

It's for this reason that it is essential to develop your own vision of what you want to create with your life. And this isn't something you do once: it requires time and energetic investment. See it in your mind every single day. Talk to yourself in the mirror with enthusiasm and unshakeable confidence.

When you're getting ready in the mornings, chat about how *great* and *easy* it was to bring your vision to fruition! Pretend you are sitting with Oprah and you're telling her about how you got it all done. Interview yourself and please feel free to *dazzle yourself* with your absolute brilliance, charisma, and joie de vivre! In fact: I insist upon it!

YOU HAVE TO LIVE BY THE PHILOSOPHY OF STRETCHING YOURSELF

What if you made the commitment to always be pushing yourself outside of your comfort zone? Now, some people would make a face if you suggested this to them... But you are not like them. You are someone who craves an exceptional life, and that means you need to do *exceptional things!*

We can all live a safe, comfortable, and stable life if that's what we desire. But why not go bigger than that?

Think about it: if you made a commitment to always go bigger and do new things, how much would your life change, flourish, evolve and up-level in a year? Five years? Ten years?!

I meant what I said at the beginning of this chapter. If I want you to really go for it, I have to do it first! I am in a massive phase of stepping it up and it feels SO GOOD! In many ways, it is scary! I have certainly had thoughts like, 'I wonder who this will annoy. I wonder who this will trigger. How will my life change if I continue on this track? Who will I have to leave behind?' Those are big questions and they are not always fun or easy to consider.

But we cannot stay where we are just to please a few people. We cannot play small because we are trying to avoid upsetting the easily offended. The truth is that those people would come up with an excuse to be upset anyway, so we have to let go of people pleasing.

"There are people that are projecting their fears and their shortcomings and failures on you. You have to be very careful with that, people telling you, 'You can't do that.' Why can't I? 'Cause they may have tried or they don't believe that they can do it. It's not really about you. It's about what they feel and their fear inside. So you have to be strong enough and resilient enough to believe in whatever it is you're trying to do." —Jay-Z

DON'T HESITATE

"If the muse comes to your bedside, don't tell her you'll fuck her later." —Allen Ginsberg

This is one of my all-time favorite quotes from the late, great Allen Ginsberg, famed beat poet. There are a few things we can do to screw up the momentum and goodness in our lives, and one of them is *hesitating*!

Hesitating doesn't always look the way we think it does. Many of us hesitate without realizing it. These are all examples of hesitation: asking everyone else for their opinion, doing endless amounts of research, refusing to commit to things, changing our minds, not returning emails or phone-calls, not writing down our ideas, and the list goes on.

Realistically, this is all self-sabotage. Nothing more, and nothing less.

We hesitate because we are afraid of failing. We hesitate because we are afraid of succeeding. We are afraid of making commitments, of making the wrong choice. We are afraid of being criticized or judged. We are afraid of embarrassing our family—by being too good or by not being good enough. And so, at a subconscious level, we think, 'If I just put this off, I won't have to deal with all these painful emotions. I won't have to disappoint anyone or stick out too much.' Oh, there are so many reasons why we hesitate.

But when we hesitate, we kill our momentum. The joy slows down. We open the car door while we're in motion and we put our feet on the ground. We create drag. We kill the excitement. We are filled with anxiety. And it takes longer to get to where we want to go.

What can you do about dismantling your urge to hesitate? You can take a look at yourself and make an inventory of all your fears. You can start to get to the bottom of why you're holding back. And then you can tap it out, baby.

IT DOESN'T TAKE A LOT OF CHANGE, JUST CONSISTENCY

As you are learning, you don't have to work really hard to change your life. It's just about making a couple of tweaks that work, and then sticking with it.

I first started my blog back in 2006, with a big vision (for me) at the time: I wanted it to be a business, and I wanted it to sustain me. The vision was great, but I was absolutely plagued by self-doubt. Every time I went to post or share something, I was overcome with feelings of unworthiness, and constantly questioned whether it was okay for me to speak up! However, instead of letting those feelings and fears tackle me and take me down, I decided I would tap on *everything that came up.*

If you've ever started a business or made a foray into entrepreneurship, you know how challenging that can be! It dredges up every fear and insecurity you've ever had, as well as plenty of new ones. So as you can imagine, I was tapping five or six times a day!

As I released old fears, and tapped in new, empowering beliefs, my business *exploded.* Within just a few months of starting my blog, I had been offered a column in *Cosmopolitan* magazine. I was receiving huge packages of clothing from advertisers. And I was invited to a fashion brunch in New York City hosted by Louis Vuitton. All of these things were huge for me!

Would all of these things have happened if I hadn't been tapping out all my resistance and fear? Maybe, but I doubt it. It's much more likely that I would have been hiding under my covers, too paralyzed with fear to keep pushing forward!

I wasn't the only person who started a blog in 2006, but the number of people who threw in the towel is enormous. They got scared, they got discouraged, they couldn't see a way to innovate and so they quit. There is so much success to be had when you just *stay in the game!*

This is why I say that consistency is key. Be consistent with working towards what you want. Be consistent with your healing. Be consistent with your self-care. Be consistent with feeling good! You will become the best version of yourself before you know it.

CELEBRATE EVERY TIME YOU DO SOMETHING GREAT

Another way to keep your energy really high is to actually—shock, horror!—celebrate your successes! Many of us simply do not do this, and after a while, it really starts to grind us down.

If you are working with passion and purpose (doesn't that sound better than "working hard"?), hitting your goals and doing it big, it is essential to take a moment to whoop it up and mark those special occasions!

I see this problem crop up a lot, especially with highly-accomplished, ambitious individuals. They are always on to the next thing, chasing the next goal, eyes on the horizon... And while it's great to be driven, to be excited, to be pulled by our dreams, it is also vital that we take a moment to *enjoy*.

As you know from the previous chapters, often it is not the moment of attaining the goal that is the part that feels best. More often, it is the journey and the trip there that was really special. So if you get to the end and it doesn't feel like much, it will create a sort of psychic drag that will hold you back—just a little bit—from doing the next big thing. If you stack enough of those moments together, you will find your ambition truly does start to wane!

Your celebrations don't have to be anything huge: simply do something that's pleasurable to you. Take an hour-long bath, sing along to your favorite album at the top of your lungs, go out with your best friend for a celebratory drink, or buy yourself a Bentley if you're feeling sassy! Who cares! Just do something that feels good to you in the moment.

In life, there are only a few times that we really allow ourselves to go all out and celebrate with the people around us: weddings, birthdays, sporting events... And maybe on rollercoasters! The coolest thing is that we can get ourselves into those peak states whenever we want! So why not tie those great feelings into accomplishing something equally great?

IT ONLY COUNTS AS PERSONAL GROWTH IF YOU DON'T WANT TO DO IT

Some of us have this idea that self-love and personal growth is just about doing the things that we want to do. You know, taking bubble-baths and stuff. And while it is important to take care of ourselves, the real growth comes when we do the things that we are not relishing.

Like when we have the uncomfortable conversations that we'd rather avoid for another year. When we state the boundary, awkward as it is, and we continue to reinforce it. When we walk away from the relationship that is not a match. When we make a commitment to fitness.

No one really wants to do these things! We would *all* rather stay where it is comfortable. Our brains are wired this way!

But when we take risks and we do the things that we know will be good for us, our energy increases. Our self-esteem goes up. And our life improves immeasurably.

MAGICAL MORNING MUST BE A DAILY DISCIPLINE

I'm so glad that we started talking about the Magical Morning Practice way back at the beginning of this book, because by now, some of you will have been doing it for a while! In that time, you will have experienced so many changes, seen so many manifestations come to fruition, and also—probably—hit a couple of plateaus!

With everything that we commit to—whether it is fitness, a relationship, a business, or a morning practice—we are going to hit a plateau at some point. We are going to reach a place where we feel like things aren't progressing, or maybe they even seem to be going backwards!

This can be incredibly frustrating, especially after you've put so much work in. You start thinking, 'Damn, has this been the best use of my time? Should I have been doing something else? What if it never gets better? What if it gets worse?!'

Feeling that sense of self-doubt is actually *part of the process*. It is an essential piece of commitment. Commitments don't come easily: they get tested!

We get tested to see how serious we are. We get tested to see if we're really in it. And surviving that test—acing it and moving through it—is part of the growth. It propels us to the next level!

I remember a while back I was dating someone and after a couple of months of it being fairly non-committal and low-stress, we had decided to step it up. We decided to be exclusive and make it a priority. I felt really good about my decision. I was stoked. Of course, two days later, I was in a restaurant when a celebrity I had been attracted to for years asked for my number! Oh, universe!

Do you know what I did in this moment? I told him NO. I told him I had a boyfriend!

"I'm not going to give you my number," I said, "But you can follow me on Instagram!"

He laughed uproariously. True story!

But I was *committed* to the decision I had made, even though the Universe had thrown me the most amazing test!

The tests that we come up against are part of the growth process. So what we have to do when they arise is to continue building our practice. If you have been doing the Magical Morning Practice and feeling some resistance, this is the time to *double down* on it! This is the time to recommit yourself to it.

Our growth is continual and it is never over. When you feel challenged, continue to move through it! Quitting on yourself will not feel good. Breathe, practice gratitude, and keep going. You've got this. ✳

11

QUESTIONS & ANSWERS

Y OU'RE ALMOST AT THE FINAL CHAPTER, AND I HAVE to say, as I wrote this book, I completely reshaped my life. As much as I was writing this for you, I was also *living* the lessons as I wrote them... And I can say with no hesitation that this is the happiest I have ever been in my entire life.

I live in a beautiful house in Orange County with a view of the ocean. I'm completely in love with and devoted to my man, who truly treats me like a queen. My dogs bring me so much joy and laughter. My body is healthy and getting stronger every day. My friends light me up and we have so much fun together. My business is booming, it's really fun to work on, and it's never been more lucrative.

Sometimes people look at other people and wrinkle their noses. "How did she get so lucky?" they ask. They chalk it up to luck, or a trust fund, or a wealthy husband. (How insulting!) Then they go back to their own life, which they hate.

When we diminish other people's accomplishments, what we are really doing is making excuses for ourselves.

If you think Max is only doing well because of connections he gained through his father, it allows *you* to take your foot off the gas. In your mind, you put them into another category. You and Max are different, his advantages were clearly unfair, and you will never have them. Based on this so-called truth, you will never be where he is, and you will never be as successful as him, so why should you even bother?

Comparison is a trap and it has many pitfalls, but the biggest is that *it stops us from even attempting to do something great.*

I can't speak for our metaphorical Max, but in my own case, here is what I can say with absolute certainty.

I have designed my life this way, and I've been doing it since 2006. I have had many lean years and times when I considered getting a second job just so I could keep writing and actually have some pocket money. People have told me not to do things—save your money! Don't hire more people! Don't branch out into this or that!—and to do plenty of other things—do collaborations with X or Y! Stay with your husband! ... The list goes on.

But I have always known exactly what I want my life to look and feel like. As you've learned from this book, plenty of that intel came from the times when my life was painful or difficult! I *know* that I want freedom to create, and that I will continue creating no matter how much money I make, because it's not about that for me. I *know* that I want to speak to huge crowds and write many, many books. I *know* what my dream house looks like! And I will not accept excuses from myself, or bow to the more "practical," well-intentioned people I may come into contact with.

Only you have to live with the choices you make. I have chosen to make bold declarations and to live an uncommon life. And truly, it feels good to do so.

It has taken a lot of time, and it has even taken sacrifice, particularly when I first started. When I lived in Melbourne, Australia, my boyfriend and I considered it a "treat" and a good day if we could afford to get lattes and bagels from the place downstairs. I could have easily gotten a job in a call center and been able to afford all the lattes and bagels I wanted... But I knew where that road led. I was so in love with my work that I would have made those same sacrifices several times over. To me, it has all been worth it.

Today, I am even more in love with my life and my work than I was back then. In 2006, I had a blog that I worked on in my living room. Now, from those very humble beginnings, I get to show up and be myself every day, and as a result, I have impacted millions of women.

As I have grown, my business has grown, and my vision has grown too. It has taken time, and is the project of a lifetime.

So next time you look at someone and feel sour because you're not where they are yet, remember that there's no such thing as an overnight success. People are rewarded in public for what they do in private. No one sees all the energy and dedication that goes into creating something successful, they just see the glossy surface.

Even people who are talented still have to put in massive amounts of energy and practice in order to be great. Don't make the popular mistake of assuming that anyone has it "easy." We all have our own struggles and we all need to put in the work to get to the peak.

✻ ✻ ✻

This book started off as an e-book, released monthly. One of the coolest things about writing it this way was that I was getting such incredible feedback from my audience while I was putting it together! For this chapter, I asked them where manifesting was tripping them up. Here are some of my favorite questions, and answers that I hope will help you!

❤ Can you be too greedy? Asking for too much?

I believe there's no such thing as long as you're bringing value and joy to others.

We are all here for a reason, and that reason is not the mindless accumulation of money and possessions. We are a collective, and we all play an essential part in uplifting the group. While money and possessions might be a pleasant side-effect of the work you do in serving the group, they are not the point... And anyone who has doggedly and single-mindedly pursued these things often comes to this realization too late.

If you want to be more successful, the answer is very simple: help more people. Bring more value. Have a bigger impact on a greater number of people.

Some people think musicians and athletes are paid too much, but ask yourself: how much joy does their work bring to the human race? Think about how the club explodes when a great song starts playing, or how an entire city can erupt ecstatically when their team wins!

People who create great works of art, who motivate others, who show us what is possible, who create a SPARK in others, are rewarded for it. Now, this is not to say you have to become a superstar to get what you want. You simply start where you are, and ask yourself every day, "Who can I help and how can I do it even better than yesterday?"

No matter who you are, we all start small. We all begin with a little idea, looking through a tiny peephole into the future and what is possible. Don't get tripped up on what is available to you right now: just take the first step, follow the divine impulses you receive, and be helpful.

The Universe will always reward you for pouring hot energy and sweetness into the world and onto the people around you. Just remember that you need to give that hot energy and sweetness to yourself first.

❤ How can we desire more and be grateful at the same time?

This is a great question because I know that this can seem like a paradox! But the truth is that we are easily able to feel good and also want more simultaneously. It happens exactly this way in many areas of our lives.

For example, you (probably) don't go to school because you think you are stupid. You go to school to build on the accumulated knowledge you already have, and get better.

We are able to be deeply appreciative of what we have experienced thus far, and also be excited for more. In fact, we cannot help but do this! Desire is the very reason we are alive. *Everyone* wants more. More love, more joy, more money, more experiences, more transcendence, more knowledge... More, more, more!

The appreciation part tends to be more difficult for people, simply because we often forget about our own bounty when we are seeking a spicy new treasure. But as you know, appreciation is a practice, it's something that you get better at over time, and it's also something which feels even more outrageously good the more that you do it.

We are all at different places in our lives. Desire is universal, but there is a lot of variety in how we get to it. Some people want more because they feel like they don't have enough, and some people want more because it is a natural expansion of their joy.

The problem with the people who want more because they feel like they don't have enough is that *we all already have everything we will ever need*. We live in a deliciously abundant Universe and there are gifts, opportunities, and resources around us at all times. If you cannot be grateful for what you have now, nothing will ever be enough.

Desiring more is easy. Being grateful takes a little more focus, but the good news is that it's really fun to practice!

❤ How do I uplevel what I believe is possible?

First of all, I want you to realize that life is a journey and a process, and in saying that, my goal is to make you understand that you don't need to come out of the womb imagining all the things that you will be capable of at 40, 60, or 80 years old.

Think about a time when you first started learning something new. Maybe it was painting, or dancing, or interior decorating. When you began, you might have had some grand ideas of what it could be, but most of the time, you don't know what's possible because *skills build upon themselves*. You would not have known this or that was achievable because you had no awareness of skills X, Y, and Z that build to it!

So what I am saying to you is that if right now, you can only see a little distance in front of you, that's okay. It's perfectly normal. *And* there are also ways to expand your vision which you will enjoy!

1. Go on joyful contemplative walks. These are my absolute favorite way to start generating delicious new ideas, and best of all, they're free. Just set off in one direction, and keep your phone in your bag as much as possible. Take in the sights and sounds. Allow yourself to get immersed in the beauty and the weirdness. You can also think of this as a walking meditation. It works brilliantly because the stimulus is constantly changing, and since you are using your whole *body*, the ideas tend to come thick and fast. You never know what you will see on a walk, or the people you will encounter. The vast majority of my best ideas have popped up while I was walking.

2. In order to get new ideas, we need new input. One of the most positive paths to this is to watch documentaries about amazing people through history. Often we feel energetically heavy because of the type of company we keep. Shedding these old connections in favor of happier, healthier ones can take some time, and can also feel a little lonely, so as you go through that process, I cannot recommend documentaries highly enough. They will expose you to new types of people, different ways of thinking, challenges you'd never imagined, and lifestyles you may have never dreamed of. This is a fantastic way to expand your vision of what is possible!

3. Get out of your house as much as you can. You can only dream so big when you're in the same spot with the same people all the time. Go to a different coffee shop every week and see who you meet. Join a co-working space and make friends. Interacting with different people who see the world in their own unique way will help you to zoom out and see the world differently, too.

4. Give yourself time and space to dream. It's hard to have new ideas when your brain is constantly on the go. Let yourself daydream, take long baths, and talk to your friends just because it feels good.

5. Spend time with people who are striving for more. This is one of the most potent ways that we can upgrade our vision. In the last year I have been exposed to many new people who are really excited about life and really committed to doing big things, and it has helped me to amp up my imagination... And as a result, the actions I take! It can take some time to meet these people, but personal development seminars or workshops are truly one of the top places to be introduced to people who are in alignment with your best self.

❤ How do I manifest my desired physical appearance?

What a yummy question! A lot of people would swear up and down that your genes are your destiny, but a cursory look at the world of epigenetics shows us that this is simply not true.

Again, it comes back to that dance between the work we do in the physical world and the work we do in the metaphysical world.

The best example I can give you of this is when I decided I really wanted to grow my butt! This might sound like a strange goal, but honey, I wanted to fill out a catsuit, so it had to be done!

In the physical world, I did everything I could to create change. I massively increased my calorie intake, and I committed to a new personal trainer. I told him what my goals were, and we set about making it happen. And here's an essential part of the story: I went about it *joyfully*. I had fun with the process! I really liked my trainer and looked forward to seeing him, and we laughed through each session.

In the metaphysical world? *I pictured all the calories I ate going to my ass.* Yes, it's true! I celebrated my body as I was going through the process, getting excited about even the smallest amount of gain or whenever I increased the weight I was lifting. I envisioned myself in the body that I wanted to have, *while at the same time* being deeply satisfied with how I looked in the present moment. I would admire my little gains and shake what I had (so far) in the mirror and laugh.

We all have different goals or aspirations when it comes to what we want our bodies to look like. In addition to visualizing and having fun with the process, I recommend hypnosis. My dear friend Grace Smith has many recordings online that can help you to rewire your brain so that you make better choices.

You can't visualize your way to a different body if you are not willing to put in the effort in the real world. But combining consistent work with a clear vision is unbelievably powerful.

❤ How do I grow more as an entrepreneur without going into more debt, or relying on family or gifts?

This is a fabulous question. A lot of us believe that in order to do the work we're here to do, we need to go really big! That's a great impulse, but it's not necessary in the beginning! You don't want to go from seedling to enormous oak tree, because you won't be ready. There is so much to learn in those beginning stages which give us the foundation and knowledge that is essential to growing and being really impactful.

The most important thing to focus on as an entrepreneur is to *provide more value*. Ask yourself, 'How can I be more valuable to my customers today? What could I give them that no one else can? How can I delight them—and myself—at the same time?'

As Derek Sivers writes in his brilliant business book *Anything You Want*, "Watch out when anyone (including you) says he wants to do something big, but can't until he raises money. It usually means the person is more in love with the idea of being big-big-big than with actually doing something useful. For an idea to get big-big-big, it has to be useful. And being useful doesn't need funding."

My advice: don't worry about growing. Just focus on being helpful, solving more problems. When you do this, the Universe cannot help but reward you. This has been so true in my own life, and I know it will be true for yours too.

❤ **Do you subscribe to the idea of getting tests from the universe? I'd love some examples of how it shows up.**

The Universe isn't testing you, but it is presenting you with the chance to practice what you say you believe!

When I say this, what I mean is: it's easy to have all the faith in the world when things are going well and you're in the vortex every day. It's a little dicier to stay focused on what you want when things appear to be going sideways!

For example, you might be telling yourself—and anyone who will listen—that the next person you get into a relationship with will be your partner for life. You visualize it, you talk out loud to your not-quite-here-yet partner when you're alone in your house, you review the list of 30 qualities that they have (and that you are so grateful for), you are working on a playlist for them that you know they will love.

And yet, at the same time... You might be going on dates with people that are simply not lighting you up. They are not bad people, you're just not feeling that ZING that you know your person will give you!

This can be super-challenging and very frustrating. You might be tempted to throw in the towel; claim that you're "over it"; shut down your dating apps and retire to bed with your sex toys forever! Who could blame you?!

Except... Doing this will not get you the result that you desire. Your dream boo isn't going to slide down the chimney like Santa Claus!

You know what you want and even though right now, the evidence might be to the contrary of that, the work is to maintain your focus. To pay attention to the things you like about these people when you go on dates, even if you know they're not your person. To be happy to go on dates at all. To continue being active in the world, putting your energy out there, and vibrating at your highest level so you can attract someone wonderful.

Being single is a fabulous opportunity to work on your own frequency and get used to regulating your energy and emotions without someone else's input. Often, in relationships, we get comfortable using the other person to bounce off. If we feel sad, we go and get a hug; if we're frustrated, we vent our frustrations with (or sometimes at) them; if we're happy, we use them to amplify it. However, when you spend prolonged periods of time by yourself, you realize that you are truly in control of how you feel, and you become the queen of it!

This is such valuable practice. It doesn't just help you to maintain your own emotional and energetic vibration when you get into a relationship, it also assists in attracting someone who is in a similarly healthy and self-contained place.

As Abraham-Hicks says, "The Law of Attraction cannot bring you a well-balanced, happy person if you are not yourself already that. The Law of Attraction, no matter what you do or say, will bring to you those who predominantly match the person who you predominantly are. ... People are often eager to find their mate immediately, even though they are not currently feeling good about themselves. They even believe that finding a mate is the path to feeling better about themselves. However, the Law of Attraction cannot bring them someone who will appreciate them when they are not already appreciating themselves. It defies Law."

As you can see, these are not "tests" exactly, but they are invitations to step up and truly do the work of loving ourselves, of believing that we can have what we want, of breathing deeply, brushing ourselves off, and taking the next step.

♥ How do I keep up positive energy if I've grown up and still live in poverty? I'm trying hard.

First of all, become aware of the language you're using. The word "try" presupposes failure, as we've covered!

Undoubtedly, some of us are in environments that support our growth, while others of us are in a place of struggle. When we look around, we see things that fill us with fear, that keep us feeling small and stuck. But the good news is that we can put ourselves in a powerful energetic state no matter what our surroundings might be signaling.

If you are not doing the Magical Morning Practice as outlined in Chapter 1, start with that. Make it a true practice: do it every single day. It will set you up for the day, and slot you into position as the potent creator of your life, as opposed to a reactor.

Start tapping on any of the limiting beliefs you have. If you're not sure what to say, it's okay to repeat yourself over and over until you feel a shift. You might start with, "I'm never going to get out of poverty" or "I don't know anything other than poverty." This will help to shift you out of fear at a subconscious level, so that you can see new solutions and possibilities.

Read up on people who were disadvantaged and went on to do incredible things. Their stories will blow your mind and help you to realize that *you can do it too.*

Finally, do whatever you can to begin associating with new types of people. Often, our community of family and friends can be the biggest roadblocks to a new life, especially when they are scared and feel lost or hopeless. Start to spend your free time in new places where you will meet other types of people.

Making changes like this can feel uncomfortable and difficult at times, but I encourage you to do things that your future self will thank you for. Any time we do something different, we are creating new neural pathways which we have never traversed before! It feels very weird and awkward to do this, like trying to write backwards. But the more that you do it, the easier and more normal it will feel!

♥ **I'm 37 and still have crippling shyness and self-doubt. How do I overcome this?**

The only things holding *any* of us back are the beliefs we hold and the stories we tell ourselves.

Here's my question for you. Is it serving you to continually tell yourself that you are limited in this way?

When I was living in Los Angles and going on dates, I went out on a date with an anesthesiologist. He was extremely smart (as one would hope!) and he had an accent that made him sound like a villain in a Bond movie. One of the highlights of the evening was him using the word "Mephistophelean" and both of us laughing. It was cute!

All was well. But he kept telling me, over dinner, how boring he was! Literally, whenever there was a lull in the conversation, he would say, "I'm sorry... I'm a terribly boring person."

The first time he said it, I said, "No you're not!" But as the dinner wore on, I grew tired of saying it. I started to think, 'It is not my job to prop you up in this arena.' And it was frustrating, because it simply wasn't true! We had plenty to talk about—it ended up being a four hour dinner!

But all his protestations that he was boring started to seep in. By the end of the night, I had decided—plot twist!—that he was boring. I texted him the next day to tell him I wasn't interested, but wished him all the best.

He has been telling himself that he is boring for years. He has told himself that so many times that he now tells *other* people, too. He believes his own lies and as a consequence, the people around him do too. Is the story of "I'm boring" one that is helping him... Or is it one that is holding him back?

If you no longer want to be controlled by your shyness and crippling self-doubt, stop telling yourself about them! Stop making these things a central part of your personality. Start to tell yourself, "Every day, I am becoming more confident. Every day, I am going outside of my comfort zone and it feels so good! Every day, I am becoming the person I want to be."

Tap on your shyness. Tap on your self-doubt.

Additionally, sit down and seriously ask yourself, 'What will my life look like in 5 or 10 years if I do not change this?' What opportunities will you miss out on? What chances will you let go? What evolution or up-leveling will you have avoided because you were simply afraid? Let this nightmarish potential future fuel your desire to change and make progress!

♥ When I have invested so much and am confronted with failure, how do I move forward?

This is a brilliant question because when you have poured a lot of your time, energy, and desire into a project (or even a person), it can be truly gut-wrenching to see that it is not going the way you want it to go.

I completely empathize with your pain and I know that everyone reading does too. Failure is universal. It is something we all experience, and it can dredge up so many uncomfortable emotions.

However, when I look back on my so-called failures, I see them as massive fountains of knowledge. The business ideas that didn't truly get off the ground, the relationships that imploded, the friendships that turned sour... I can see the reason why these things didn't work out, and that gives me such valuable data, as well as a clear roadmap of what to avoid in the future!

You may be too close to the failure right now to see the gems within it, but I promise that they are there, and with time, these will become abundantly clear.

To deal with it in the moment, ask yourself, 'What about this project didn't work for me? What about it didn't work for others? What was great about it? What was terrible about it?' Appraise it honestly.

You may not have to give it up entirely, either. What would happen if you gave up on your idea of how it should be, and instead started to pay attention to how things are shifting? Maybe you don't have to give up the ghost entirely—maybe it could take a new form or shape and still be deeply pleasurable or satisfying. What could that look like?

But it might be something that you cannot—or do not want to—salvage. In that case, you may need to grieve the project. Throw it a little funeral. Allow yourself to feel sad and devastated and let your feelings wash over you. Don't punish yourself. This failure could very well have been a blessing in disguise (and they often are).

Then, when you're ready, new inspiration will come. Ideas will form all by themselves. And you will be on to the next thing. That's just how life works.

♥ When I have anxiety I freak out because I automatically think I'm manifesting something bad, which as you can imagine, makes it worse. How do you combat this?

This is such a commonly-held belief, so I'm really glad you asked this question! Many of us have bought into the story that if we "think a bad thought," we are instantly creating tragedies in our real lives. It's kind of like that scene in *Amelie* where, as a little girl, her neighbor tells her that using a camera causes accidents, and after a day of snapping photos, Amelie watches the news, horrified to think that she has caused five-car pile-ups and forest fires! The good news is that—just like Amelie discovered—this is categorically not how it works.

After all, if it did work that way, people all around you would be dying sudden deaths because you shot them an evil look! (On the plus side, it would bring a swift end to cat-callers!)

You know that your mind is powerful and you also know that thoughts become things. The good news is that it doesn't happen instantly!

Even when I teach people about tapping, sometimes they get nervous because they think that speaking their fears out loud will cause them to come to fruition. Tapping is not like talk therapy—where you repeat your fears over and over for years!—it is about acknowledging what you fear so that you can bring it up and literally remove the thought from your consciousness. It is like removing an emotional thorn from your body.

The truth is that we need to acknowledge our fears in order to remove them. Denying what we are afraid of never works, and the fear simply burrows deeper and deeper, gaining traction and strength. Even worse, sometimes then the fear warps and starts coming out in weird and unexpected ways.

If anxiety is something that you struggle with, I truly cannot recommend tapping highly enough. Simply tapping on the points while you talk about your anxiety, what it is about, where you feel it in your body and how it feels, will be massively impactful.

I have worked with so many people who once suffered from crippling anxiety and now it is not even a part of their life. Anxiety, depression, eating disorders, or anything else that you once considered a life sentence simply does not have to be. I implore you to try tapping. I believe it will change your life for good.

❤ **What does staying "high vibe" actually mean to you? Cause it would be impossible for a human to truly be happy, feeling good, and feeling in flow all day every day... Right?**

To me, staying high vibe is about being in control of my emotional frequency. It means that when I notice I am backsliding into an unpleasant thought or engaging in activities that feel energetically gross, I do something to remedy it as soon as I can.

Sometimes that can be a challenge because it feels comfortable to be in that low vibe place! Sometimes we almost enjoy those surly thoughts and that angry vibe. But it doesn't lead us to a place that feels truly good, so we want to catch it and ACT our way into a better feeling place!

This may shatter your illusions about what is possible but I am—as you say—truly happy, feeling good, and feeling in flow every day, for at least 80% of it. Maybe even 90%. No exaggeration.

Here's what you should know about this.

My feeling so good, with such regularity, and such consistency, is a *product of my practices.* Those practices are primarily tapping, exercise, and making feeling good my priority. And for me, historically, living alone helps with this too!

You may be in a place right now where you seldom interact with people who feel good. Of course if this is your situation, you will assume that no one could truly be happy all day! We believe what we see and we believe what we tell ourselves. Even the way that you phrased your question indicates massive disbelief and skepticism!

The more that you work on yourself, and the more that you come into alignment, the more you will attract people who feel good, just like you are starting to. It is like climbing a ladder, and it just gets better and better.

❤ **When you're manifesting something, and you don't feel high vibe, are you blocking it?**

Almost.

You are *always* manifesting something you want. It is always in process. As soon as you realize you want it, the Universe is already working to bring it to you. But your attitude determines how close or far away it is.

If you're in a bad mood, you are slamming the door on the thing you want. You are shooing it away. You are curled up in bed, hiding from it.

You are never fully *blocking* a manifestation in that your desire will never come to you full stop, But every surly mood, negative spiral, and angry tantrum keeps it at arm's length.

The good news is that when you get into the vortex—aka you start to feel slight joy, then pleasure, then deep joy, then ecstasy—the things you want rush towards you with such speed! ✳

12

IT ALL COMES TOGETHER

C REATION IS EASY. IT HAPPENS IN AN INSTANT. THE essential elements of manifesting are as follows...

♥ EXPERIENCE CONTRAST

These are the things that you don't like. This could range from a painful relationship to a medical emergency, burn-out in your career to realizing you don't trust any of your friends. Yes, this will probably hurt, but it will expand your vision so that you become acutely aware of what you want!

♥ FEEL INSPIRATION

This is when you experience desire. When inspiration or desire strikes, it is undeniable. You will feel the flutter of it, a flutter which pushes you towards something equal parts undefinable and exciting. The more you pay attention to these flutters, the more often they will occur.

♥ ACT UPON THAT INSPIRATION

This is where the rubber meets the road, or the metaphysical meets the physical. The Universe has called upon you to do something new, and now you use your body to honor that request. Maybe you make a phone call, maybe you have a courageous conversation, maybe you make a plan or book a plane ticket.

♥ DISCARD WHAT IS NO LONGER IN ALIGNMENT

This can take many shapes. It could be that you utilize tapping to remove the emotional thorns that are holding you back, or it could be cleaning out a closet. It might be quitting a job, leaving a relationship or changing your hair.

♥ ENJOY THE PRESENT MOMENT WITH YOUR ENTIRE BEING

No matter where you are in the process of manifesting, it is absolutely essential to feel good about it. To have faith in it. To truly love the journey so much that *you get to the point where it doesn't matter whether the final product manifests or not.*

♥ MANIFESTATION!

Ding ding ding!

♥ ...BACK TO STAGE 1!

When I reflect on all the times I have had success with my manifestations, it has been as a result of first noticing that something wasn't working, and then following these steps.

This strategy has worked to make my business more lucrative and joyful than ever before, to enhance my relationships, to deepen my friendships, and to uplevel my health.

The more that I practice these steps, the less dramatic my life becomes. In fact, it would be fair to say that in my life, stress is a rare occurrence! I have let go of the friendships that don't feel good, the habits that were bumming me out and the beliefs that were holding me back.

As I step away from drama and chaos, I look less upon my life as a puzzle to solve, but instead as a beautiful canvas to play on. I observe the landscape and I ask myself, "How can I amplify or maximize this?" Imagine a beautiful piece of music on the board at a recording studio, with never-ending dials and buttons that can be tweaked, pushed, and played with. That is what my life feels like.

I am constantly looking at the various areas of my life and asking myself, "How can I have more fun?"

That is the question that guides my life these days.

When I ask myself this, my life unfurls in front of me like a big beautiful flower, or a magical Moroccan carpet, or the tongue of God. The answer becomes clear, and I simply follow my bliss.

Writing a book makes you contemplate the vastness of your own life, and sometimes one of the most eye-opening ways of doing that is scrolling back through old photos on your phone. Last night, I felt inspired to go through pictures from my final days in New York, just before I moved to Los Angeles. It was such a time of radical growth! I saw a picture of myself where I was staring wide-eyed at the camera, high on possibility and excited to see what the Universe had in store. I remember feeling free and hopeful and inspired, and of course, that inspiration nudged me forward into my next incredible chapter.

At the time, I was loving my life in a whole new way, stretching my wings and tasting the world. After a decade in New York City, I felt strongly that our love affair was over. I had been obsessed with New York even before I'd touched down there, and when I moved to the city in 2008, I fell head-over-heels. It was my crush for a long time. But at the ten year mark, I was ready for something different. New York City and I hadn't had a lover's quarrel or even a mild falling-out. I just knew that we were complete... And that Los Angeles was calling me.

I packed a suitcase with wigs, crystals, bedazzled high heels and sneakers (only the essentials, you understand), and boarded a one-way flight from New York to Los Angeles. I didn't totally know what I wanted or what I expected, I was simply following stage directions from the universe.

The first place I stayed in Los Angeles was between two neighborhoods, up a hill and in the middle of nowhere. I had picked it because of the outdoor space—which I eventually made very good use of—but I had a moment of New York-esque panic the first night because I didn't know where to get food! In NYC, you just walk outside and there are a million places to eat. In LA, not so much! Thankfully, I asked someone what to do and he pointed me to a food delivery app. Phew! Crisis averted!

There were many small differences between the coasts. In New York City, there is always a siren wailing, loud motorcycle pipes, someone playing a radio underneath your window, or a neighbor hanging pictures at 2am. Los Angeles is still and silent at night, and especially so in a neighborhood. In hotels, there is always some noise: a neighbor, a cart rolling past, housekeeping knocking on the door. In an Airbnb, especially at night, it could be hauntingly quiet. The first night I found it eerie, but soon I relished the silence. It felt good. I slept peacefully and woke up to blue skies every morning.

Every week, I would re-pack my suitcase and roll off to a new location, a different neighborhood every time. My goal? To find a neighborhood in Los Angeles that I loved.

In August, a friend asked me, "Are you looking for places to live?" I told her no, and then realized that maybe I should! I started looking at rental properties loosely, in no rush, because I was still paying rent in New York City. I went to look at one house, but it didn't feel quite right. I shrugged and kept looking at listings.

A couple of days later, I saw a listing that almost made my heart stop. As soon as I clapped eyes on it, I knew that it was my place. I showed up to the open house, and as I walked through the space, I couldn't help but notice the scent of palo santo. I approached the real estate agent and said, "I like the palo santo!"

She smiled at me and opened her palm, which contained a collection of crystals. "Thank you!," she said. "I'm trying to attract some good energy today."

Needless to say: she found it.

Before I knew it, I was rolling my suitcase in the front door. I bought an inflatable mattress and slept on the floor with my laptop and a chilled bottle of Perrier Lime. The house was completely empty but I was overjoyed, so excited about my new life, and waking up every day feeling so blessed.

That's how it works. Manifesting is always kick-started by feeling contrast, then inspiration, and taking a leap of faith. I flew to Los Angeles because I felt like

I needed to be there. Abraham would call this "inspired action," where you feel the call to do something and then you act upon it.

And I have had this same situation play out in my life so many times. I have noticed that something is dissatisfying, I have created rockets of desire, and then I have taken inspired action that leads me to something incredible.

Following your inspiration and taking action is not for the faint of heart. When you do this, there are no guarantees. You don't know what is waiting for you on the other side, but you decide to trust in life and in yourself and you do it anyway.

Now that I had my new house in Los Angeles, it was time to clear out my belongings in New York. My best friend Shauna flew with me to New York so we could clean out my old apartment and kiss it all goodbye. One night, I had the idea to post my address online and have a huge sale... So we did!

The sale was incredible. Before we opened my front door, we heard some commotion, peeked out the window, and saw a line of women lined up down the street! As the day progressed I met some wonderful people. I felt so much joy watching them try on my old Betsey Johnson dresses and the jewelry I had spent a decade collecting. Shauna and I started the day with a house full of stuff. By the end of the day, we didn't even have a couch to sit on!

We performed a total exorcism on that place before we dragged the mattress down the stairs, slid the key under the mat, and left it behind forever.

Getting rid of the physical items that had tied me to New York and to my old life was a ritualistic letting go of that which no longer felt aligned. When I returned to Los Angeles, a U-Haul pulled up outside my house containing little more than my Nespresso machine, some favorite books, and the clothes I loved. It only took me a couple of hours to put it all away: that's how little I had brought with me.

As I turn up my frequency and turn my focus to being ever more of a high vibe honey, I am discarding the things that no longer fit. I have let go of friendships that didn't feel fully supportive or healthy. I have let go of sugar. I have let go of old clothes from my past lives. I have let go of gluten! I have let go of old resentments and pain and sadness. I have let go of limiting beliefs.

And with everything that I put my energy into—from my workouts at the gym to my social life to my work—I focus with the entirety of my being. I do my best to be absolutely present. When I am with my friends, I keep my phone in my bag (for the most part!). When I am at the gym, I am not thinking about anything else. When I am creating, my vision of what I am making is all-encompassing. This sense of focus brings me delirious joy and helps me continue to build positive momentum.

Who knows where all this can lead? I have no idea, but I am delighted as it continues to unfold. And yet, at the same time, know this: if I don't wake up tomorrow, know that I lived as wonderfully as I knew how, and I truly, madly, deeply loved my life.

This book would not be complete without hearing from some of the babes who were on this journey with me, reading the chapters every month and making adjustments. When I asked how their lives had changed in the past year, the answers were wild, moving, and beautiful. Here are some of my favorite responses.

✳ ✳ ✳

Magnetic Mindset and the practices within it got me out of a toxic workplace and into a beautiful one; into higher degree research in a discipline I adore with my whole entire heart; out of a relationship I thought was going to be my life, and into a relationship with MYSELF that is more profoundly joyous, worshipful, fun and nourishing than anything I could have imagined. (And as a fun side effect, has brought me into alignment with a MEGA GORGEOUS man, previously "just" a friend, who is seriously like a human conduit for how much the Universe loves me.)

I now trust and know myself, my intuition, my heart and my power, more than I ever felt possible. I feel like a big happy love beam, I dance every day for fun, my life is full of wonderful generous loving people, and life is JUICY AS FUCK.

Thank you for integrating all these amazing practices and perspectives and also for BEING the work. I think I've said, I've been following you since 2010 and your transformation has been so profound and moving.

Zoe O'Leary Cameron

✳ ✳ ✳

Magnetic Mindset and Gala Darling have transformed my thinking and improved my entire life. The biggest difference is within my marriage. Magnetic Mindset helped me see what is possible, and my husband agreed to start marital counseling. I have finally been able to address my over-functioning tendencies and speak my truth. We are improving our communication skills and learning how to acknowledge feelings without fixing them. Listening to Magnetic Mindset every morning motivated me to dream bigger and envision new possibilities for my life. I'm continuing to retrain my thoughts and tap out old, limiting stories about him and us. It feels so good to be this hopeful and excited about our future together.

Our home is now a space of renewal and beauty. We hired a house cleaner once a month and that feels like such a gift! Walking into a perfectly clean home is the best feeling. My stress levels are way down and I'm able to relax and enjoy time with my 3-year old daughter. I also started a garden and added beautiful hanging flower baskets outside. Now my daughter loves eating kale chips from the garden every week! Gala inspired me to clean my front door with citrus essential oil and let in new opportunities. We also painted, added artwork and bought a new lamp. The entire place feels fresh and beautiful!

Additionally, Magnetic Mindset, Radical Rituals: Abundance and the Kris Jenner meditation completely transformed my finances. It blows me away to write this:

I covered another woman's maternity leave for three months and made $8000 extra dollars. This is an opportunity that I originally declined, but after listening to the Kris Jenner meditation, I reconsidered and said yes. I'm so glad I received that guidance because it was a great experience for my career and my pocket book.

Last week my intuition helped me notice an error in my work contract for next year. After correcting the error, I will be making an additional $5,000 next year. Additionally, I'll be saving more for retirement and paying less for health insurance. The ripple effects are incredible!

Gala helped me realize that abundance is more than just cash money. I started to receive and appreciate all of the gifts that flooded my way like a free barbeque, books, lunches, dahlia bulbs, gift cards and coffee. I'm feeling grateful and rich every single day. I exude confidence and see myself as a powerful, affluent woman who's in control of her life.

Finally, I booked us a magical 5-year Anniversary trip for next year in Mexico. Now I see that money equals freedom and adventure, I'm prioritizing pleasure and fun in my life and I have the financial means to make it happen. I'm so excited every day!

Throughout this entire experience, my Magical Morning partner, Sarah, has encouraged me. I contacted her using the form Gala provided, and I believe it was destiny. We've been sending audio messages and powerful texts every day. She supports me, challenges me and helps me see new ways of operating. We've met four times IRL, and I even attended her recent performance with the Transformational Women's Circus. I never would have met her otherwise, and she has become a consistent, solid, supportive, magical force in my life. Gala, I'm so grateful for this book and all of your fabulous work in this world. Thank you a thousand times over!

Nicole Perriella-Rehmke

I left an unfulfilling relationship, had a life changing surgery that removed my endometriosis pain, and have a plan to pay off my debt by the end of this year--a total of $17,000! I feel like I've leveled up during this process and that I'm not done yet, not even close.

Alisha Lovely

✳ ✳ ✳

I'm generally super hesitant about committing to anything, let alone an online penpal of sorts, but from the first few morning texts with Kate, things really started to shift. My mornings were hella chaotic, and while I had a morning routine, it frankly sucked. Kate ended up being basically a soul sister. We were definitely twins or besties in a past life. While we live only an hour apart in Wisconsin, and our paths probably crossed when we both lived in the same town years ago, there's probably no reason we would have met in this life. Holy shit, I'm so glad we did.

While we aren't always great at doing this first thing in the morning, it serves as the perfect reset in the middle or even at the end of the day to reflect with gratitude and proclaim how the rest of the day will shape up.

Fast forward a few months later, both of us were in the thick of all sorts of heavy shit, life changes, personality changes and also both in the thick of an absurdly cold Wisconsin winter. This practice literally helped each other through work, family, everything. It was about that time that we moved our texting over to Marco Polo, so we got to talking longer, more in depth, and truly sharing all the details that text just doesn't make easy.

I can't count the number of times that once I started rambling on about my gratitudes my entire day shifted dramatically. I can't count all the times that something I proclaimed in my texts to Kate happened! I can't count the number of times that Kate's response to my MM or my reading hers motivated me to hold myself to a higher standard and reframe my situation. I can't count the number of times I legitimately felt Kate's gratitude, joy, etc. I have a sounding board and a mirror in Kate. I have a total bestie in her. I get so excited to read what she's up to each day and am constantly grateful to have this practice as an anchor in my life.

Our morning texts look so different now—we talk about things that had you asked me in October if I'd be talking about with anyone, let alone someone I met from a spreadsheet from a woo woo book I was somewhat surprised I even signed on for, the answer is a hard no.

Kate is a lifer friend now. I'm so grateful to be able to share thoughts, experiences, manifestations, and play around with concepts that previously seemed too esoteric to even apply to me. We've manifested thousands of dollars that we asserted we would -probably only half-believed we'd find. We've manifested meeting people we said we would. We've manifested so much of what we've dreamed, and while we're actively still en route to some incredible things, it no longer seems scary or hard. When things aren't happening on our timeline, we so clearly reframe why that may be happening and find the growth or learning moment the Universe is trying to help us see instead. We have faith in the end-game, and we hold each other to it. Ultimately, visions seem so much more certain, attainable, and fun knowing that I'm not alone. I'm seen, heard, supported, and totally cheered on, and that's a gift I'll be forever grateful for.

Katherine Gramann

* * *

Like lots of new quests I find myself on, I hardly ever remember how I stumbled upon the thing that led me to the even bigger thing that I am speechlessly grateful for. Discovering Gala is one of those quests I truly do not remember how or why I stumbled upon her. But as soon as I watched a High Vibe Honey in July of last year—and didn't even know what tapping was (I literally just watched the video without doing a thing, lol) I knew I needed to learn everything that I possibly could from her. At the time, I wasn't familiar with manifesting, anything woo or spiritual. I barely had a routine or ritual in place—let alone a morning routine. I was coming out of a 2+ year hiatus of loving myself, and I wasn't even well versed in expressing gratitude.

So, by the time Magnetic Mindset was announced, I immediately jumped at the opportunity, without ever imagining how my life would change. I remember writing in my journal about what my life would look like in 10 months time after the last chapter of this book, and I mostly remember focusing a lot of my vision around money. But then, as I did begin to introduce tapping into my regular routine, and make time and space for the things that were serving me—I realized I didn't truly have someone to share my journey with. When the Magical Morning Practice was introduced in Chapter 1, I was hesitant at first to add my name and reach out to anyone—I waited a week, and to be completely honest I chose Katherine because I recognized the area code of her phone number (it was local to where I grew up) and that felt safe. After sharing our first Magical Morning, I immediately felt the magic.

Since October, my life has completely changed. There have been good days, great days, "holy shit is this my life" days, and then lots of "I legit want to quit life" days. But the thing that kept me going, wanting to change, wanting to evolve, grow, uplevel, and celebrate becoming the best version of myself was the Magical Morning Practice with Katherine. This bish is my legitimate bestie. Never would I have imagined receiving such an incredible person in my life, and having it take 32 years. I truly cannot even imagine my life without her. SO dramatic. Yet, so necessary.

How we share our practice hasn't changed much, but what we share has. The way I think, speak, and feel about myself, others, this planet, the universe, everything, improves every single day, and it's because of the deep level of gratitude we express. We've gone from saying "I am grateful for the sunshine" to "I am grateful for the beautiful bright sun that shines down onto mother earth and provides us with light to see during the day, and growth to the plants, flowers, trees, fruits, and vegetables."

Katherine holds me accountable, allows me to be me, and then doesn't allow me to be anything less than the goddess-like version of myself she knows I'm meant to be. Together, we have upleveled our minds, our businesses, and our lives, and all of this just in the last 8 months. She is an incredible soul and I am forever grateful for her.

Kate Killoran

✳ ✳ ✳

At the beginning of this journey I was hurting in so many areas. I was still healing from the end of my marriage, the loss of the job I was making the most money for and running my own business, on top of struggling with depression and anxiety.

Interesting enough, through this journey things kind of just kept getting worse. But it was because I had SO MUCH RESISTANCE. Truthfully, it wasn't until the last two days that this resistance has vanished. I am thankful that the Universe did what it had to do to push me out of this miserable comfort zone. My job that I've had for the last year, that I put my heart and soul into just was not flourishing at all (eight of cups from high vibe honey last week solidified that.) Along with my job, I realized my current relationship was also not doing it for me. As much as I love my boyfriend and he's taught me so much, I realized after an amazing pep talk he gave me that we had absolutely no romance. And that I truly need to be alone. I started dating him shortly after my marriage ended because he was familiar and made me feel safe. I was using everything and anyone around me to hold me up.

As of last week, I received the job offer of my dreams! An esthetician who I've been following for years, who has built an amazing brand and business all by herself has decided to expand. Apparently I was the first to send my resume and I ended up being her first choice! I was nervous about leaving the job I had been at for a year, and in that same week the vibe with my boss became unbearable that we had to part ways. Because of that I was able to network at my new job and celebrate my new boss babe's one year anniversary of her first store front. It's been one year and she's already ready to move into a bigger space! I am so excited for this project every time I think about the possibilities I bubble with joy. I am excited for the JOURNEY not just the destination.

Gala, you came into my life at such a perfect time. I've been fortunate enough to speak with you one on one and your videos and this book, even though I didn't see it all the time, kept me going when normally I would have completely given up. It's funny that at the end of this book I feel like I'm finally beginning. I thought it would be the other way around but I am so thankful for the way things played out!

Though it might not look like it in physical manifestation just yet, my life has radically transformed. I have manifested everything I've wanted and the rest is so close I can taste it! I encourage anyone who's going to read this book to stick with it, and know not everyone's timeline is the same. I thought my life would be more "together" by now from how I envisioned it at the beginning. Now that we are at the end, I realize what is happening now is SO MUCH SWEETER than my original, simple hopes and dreams. Thank you!

Carli

✳ ✳ ✳

At the beginning I was living in a place that wasn't mine, struggling to stay optimistic and although things definitely weren't terrible I knew they could be so much better. I wanted a home. I started doing the Magical Morning Practice via journaling (just because that's what I dig most), tapping on the sticky stuff and making written cases against limiting beliefs—I can't recommend this enough! Over the course of the book, things have changed significantly. I bought my very own apartment which is a dream. In fact, it's better than I ever could have imagined! My little garden is currently blooming with jasmine, roses, eucalyptus, all sorts, the colors are incredible! I've been blessed with some huge walls and high ceilings to hang the art I love, it's a sanctuary—and I love it! Now don't get me wrong—this is real life and I barely have any furniture! BUT it's a process, and what I've learned is to soak up and enjoy every moment, things are on their way—my job is just to feel good and let them come!

Helskibeat

* * *

Before embarking on the Magnetic Mindset journey, I was feeling stuck in multiple ways. I was dealing with a close friendship that had gone sour because I started realizing this friend wasn't cheering me on anymore, was jealous of the good things in my life, and I was so conflicted because I had so much love for her! This was one of the hardest things that I had to do, but because of Magnetic Mindset I raised my standards and decided after a year of being on the fence with this friend I had to let her go. Because of Magnetic Mindset, I no longer accept anyone's BS, bad behavior, or the like!

As for my big manifestation goal when I started, my goal (as if it was already real) was "I am so happy and grateful that I live in a beautiful home with my amazing, loving boyfriend and our animals. It's affordable, and close to both of our jobs. I feel amazing and inspired all the time, and the money flows to me consistently."

Up until this month, my boyfriend and I have been doing the long distance thing for one entire year, since May 2018. He lived on the west coast of Florida and I live on the east.

We sign the lease to our beautiful new apartment with a lake view this week! 10 minutes from our jobs and affordable. Everything I had wanted, manifested.

Coincidence that this is happening by the time the last chapter of Magnetic Mindset hits? I don't think so! Also, if you were wondering... Cash money is flowing FREELY and I love that I am able to donate to causes that I care about, and have money left over. I don't own my own business—I work for a non-profit in the field of wildlife conservation, but the money is ALWAYS there when I need it. I also took your abundance class too!

Overall, I am much more confident in who I am and what I'm looking for in life because of this book. I stuck with my Magical Morning Practice every day. Whether I meditated, tapped on an issue I was having, wrote out a gratitude list, and sometimes dabbled in voice notes just for myself, I was dedicated to my practice and will continue it!

Another noteworthy change in my life is that I am so much quicker to change my thoughts. I notice right away when I start going downhill and I reach for a better feeling thought! Now, I am 100% more trusting of the universe, and I know it is always working for me and protecting me from what I "think" I wanted. And I've made feeling good my priority—every. damn. day.

Shelby

✳ ✳ ✳

At the beginning of this journey I was going through the hardest situation I thought I could be. I was losing my father to cancer. I was low, lost, and incredibly depressed. Self hatred was a big thing for me at the time. After he passed I put this aside for a while, telling myself I didn't deserve to be happy. I felt that I couldn't heal. Then one day, one particular email around the third or fourth chapter I believe, I decided I was going to show up and start reading again. Now I have started to move forward in so many things in my life. I was able to climb out of a depression, learned how to move through grief and become stronger. I have started my business up again, my relationships have gotten stronger and I am starting to see each and every day as a learning experience. I feel more confident, alive and ready to live my best life ever. Not to mention I have fully enjoyed learning about tapping, connecting to others enjoying this journey, and appreciate each and every person's journey. Thank you so much for this experience.

Bex

✳ ✳ ✳

Things have really changed! I manifested my dream job where I get to work remotely and travel the world! I have been asking for what I want and am in a loving relationship where I feel safe to talk about being open and having more than one lover. Confidence coming out of me like whoa. Thank you Gala.

At the beginning of this journey I was struggling with the end of my marriage, the death of my father and soon after I lost my dog, then aunt and fell out with my closest friend. I learned so many things on this journey and my life on the outside may not look that different to others, I still go for crazy long walks and love being in the forest. Even though I have always liked to be alone, this journey totally transformed me in a beautiful way when I started to LOVE my own company. I learned that I need to set boundaries with others but more importantly with myself. And dancing when and where I want is the ultimate expression of joy and freedom to me.

I have actually been hoarding a golden goose egg that I have been working on since last August. I realized much of my happiness comes from doing things at my own pace. That putting any expectations other than feeling good on myself after the year I have been through, is just a bonus. I learned it's not just okay to grieve and work through the pain to get to a better place but absolutely necessary. I think I must have tapped about three hours a day some months and others only once a week. It really works wonderfully for me. Also I am now addicted to Perrier and will fully support them endorsing you!

I got my archaeology diploma in the winter, did tons of renovations in my house to make it nicer for me and my kids. I made appointments with an immunologist, geneticist and rheumatologist to help with my fevers, skin and arthritis so I can function more fully. Last appointment is next week. The best part is I literally burnt my past. Ok there are still a couple boxes left to burn, but it has been so therapeutic I decided to burn chunks at a time instead of all at once.

I dyed my hair pink, purple and blue just for fun, started going to museums and galleries again and reading books for pleasure. I think perhaps one of the sweetest things that happened on this journey was reconnecting with an old friend who lives on the other side of the country. She was really depressed and her 20 year marriage was about to be over. Although she didn't take this course, me including her in my Magical Morning Practice changed her life in such lovely ways. Her and her husband are doing really well together enjoying life with their kids. She called me so excited the other night because she felt so happy, was taking better care of her body, lost a ton of weight and was looking for more ways to make her life even more amazing. I felt really good to be a part of that experience and was so grateful to share her joy. We are seeing each other in August.

Thank you for being such a wonderful teacher. I now know how to keep my light shining in times of darkness so I don't feel lost. I know how to use that light to brighten the paths of others. I learned to deeply value my friendships, children and cat. More importantly, I love myself more everyday and because of that everyday is more delicious... Thank you so much. I loved being a part of this. I am going to go through it all over again once it's over. Then nothing can stop me, ever.

I love you and everything you do!

Vaise Souris

At the start of the book I felt undervalued and overworked in my career. Today I am making more than double my salary than at the start of the book (over $100k!!!). My new job has mounds of potential growth for me to step into. I was able to clear $10k of debt accumulated over the last 15 years for good. I have a savings account with more than 100 dollars in it for the first time in years. I feel more connected to myself, the people, places, and things I love spending time with. This book provided me with tools, gave me prompts and examples of how to use them and let me witness my own magic, skills, and intelligence.

Stacy S.

* * *

At the beginning of this journey, I was lost and looking for meaning. I felt absolutely stuck and like I could not get unstuck. I was constantly grasping at quick-fix and material things in an attempt to make myself feel better, more worthy, and to escape. I wanted to be spiritual, to accomplish my goals and dreams, and to really connect to people, but I had a lot of walls and defenses built up against all of that because I was scared. I remember feeling anxious and pent up about EVERY little thing. I was experiencing panic attacks and hardly ever leaving my house.

Today, I am more often at peace and continuing to learn to trust the Universe in its timing and love for me. I have learned how to get back to my center, and because of this class and many of your other videos/ teachings, I have branched out to find more and more of these types of practices to apply to my life. And I couldn't be more excited to say that I have learned how to truly ENJOY my life! It doesn't mean that I don't ever experience fear or hardship, but it does mean that I am confident in my ability to take on whatever is thrown at me. It means that I have the tools and resources to take ownership of my reality and create a life that I love and am grateful for every. single. mother-freaking. day.

I hope to one day inspire people, as you have, with my creative gifts. I am on the path to doing this now. Thank you again for your radiance, which shines so brightly and lights up this world.

Erin Vernon

At the beginning of my journey, I had these goals: pay off my house, write more books, and get paid well to speak and teach at events all over the world. I have been working on paying off the house early for some time and was facing the finish line (thank you Saturn in the 2nd house!). The house is now paid off. I have new book proposals that are about to get a yes. And the best part? I got a paid teaching event in Italy next year! Woohoo! I feel GREAT. Ready for more of this, please.

Theresa Reed

✳ ✳ ✳

Gala your books, teachings, tapping, Magnetismo, High Vibe Honey, Radical Rituals: Abundance, and Love, Example, and Belief has changed my life. Back in September I read Radical Self Love. I experienced total self love for the first time. That was the stepping stone to all my experiences with your teachings and projects. Your business model for books where you include the reading and the audio is fabulous. You reach people with different needs—auditory or visual plus when I did both it integrated it more. The business model of releasing a chapter per month for input is brilliant. Totally felt a part of a community. Your authenticity has moved me to understand authenticity. I previously thought of it as vulnerability but that shift to authenticity has made it easier for me to be that. My shift and changes have created my interaction with the world to be more loving, authentic, patient, understanding, and incredible. Loving, accepting, and forgiving myself helps me to be a better parent that loves, accepts and forgives my children without my expectation of perfection previously because I expected that from myself. My experience of tapping has changed my life. I have always been a big affirmation person. So doing all the tapping helped release blocks and integrate amazing stuff in my life. What you represent is so powerful and phenomenal and your love and support to provide self-examples and advice given but also followed by you to us so we can be the best version of ourselves and uplevel the world. I respect, admire, support, and love you and will be loyal to your future books, classes, and projects. Thank you Gala for changing my life!

Anonymous

✳ ✳ ✳

My life has completely transformed since I have found you. So my journey starts way before this chapter of Magnetic Mindset. When I was a teenager I struggled with many things like depression, anxiety, and attempted suicide. I found my way out though through therapy and self care. But then unexpectedly in September 2013, my dad passed away and it tore me apart. He was who I connected with so it really took a huge toll on me. I struggled again with depression but decided to work on myself.

Fast forward to 2017, I found you by googling self care blogs and instantly was hooked! Your energy and happiness is so inspiring! I started taking your courses and working on my radical self love.

Then again, unexpectedly in September of 2017, my mom passed away. It was extremely rough. But because of you and because of my practice of self care and all these different tools I've learned, I handled that tragedy with much more strength then I could have ever imagined.

Even when I was struggling through dealing with my loss, I left my boyfriend of 5 years because he was mistreating and controlling me, and I learned that I was worth more and couldn't stay with someone who was hurting me while I was already hurting. I also left a terrible job. All of this allowed me to become who I really wanted to be. It was painful but so freeing.

This past year and eight months has been the hardest of my life. But with help from you, I can say that I am the happiest I have ever been. I have a great job that is fun and pays well. I have a great chosen family that provides me support and love. I am so grateful for the legacy that my parents left for me and will allow me to create so many amazing things. I have so many blessings that, thanks to you, I try to count everyday. I choose to be happy everyday for myself, for others, and for my parents. They wouldn't want it any other way.

Many people don't know my story, and as soon as they find out, they always say "I would have never guessed! You are always so happy!" or things like that. Thanks to you I know I can be happy regardless of the situation. Thanks to you I have had many blessings, and have countless to come. Thanks to you I expect more from life and I dream big. Thanks to you, my life which many would think is sad and tragic, is full of love, happiness, and possibilities. I have been wanting to write to you and this chapter was perfect timing. Again, thank you for all that you do.

Jessica Judd

✳ ✳ ✳

This experience has been so awesome and I know it's far from over! At the beginning of this journey, I was just settling into being in a better place. I had started my new job as a veterinary technician at the incredible veterinary practice where I'm currently working and thriving. This was after a shitstorm of a first year living in a new town juggling multiple jobs working mostly with douchebags. I had also recently hooked up with someone after an eternal dry spell. I'm talking to the point of me being ok with never having sex with anyone every again which is a little dramatic but no sex is better than bad sex right? I was feeling pretty good, though I must say there were some growing pains from not being used to being treated well at work or given sexual attention that I actually wanted from someone I was attracted to mutually. Little did I know, this was just a baseline.

Now I feel high vibe/in control of my emotions 75% of the time. And when I start spiraling into feeling shitty, I have a toolbox of things to turn to including Buti yoga, tapping, tarot, meditative hiking, painting, kundalini meditation and jogging. I reach into that toolbox and snap myself back to happy. I still enjoy a dark sense of humor that extends to styles of clothing and music. Yet, despite what anyone may think, my taste in those things isn't indicative of me hating my life. In fact, it's just the opposite. I get to enjoy doing whatever I want, even if it seems fucked up or like too much to an outsider looking in. I adore that I'm known around town as the lady with the cat ears and purple hair! And I love embodying my feline essence unapologetically.

I feel an incredible amount of confidence to do what I want by myself if no one wants to join me. Throughout this journey I have upleveled the hell out of my relationship with myself and realized that I haven't truly met anyone worthy of giving up my solitude for (which is probably why I have only met men primarily interested in being friends with benefits/no strings attached because the time is not yet right for anything more). And that's ok! There is no rush. There is love all around me and I share beautiful connections and more intimacy than I ever have in my life with my girl gang who, fun fact, is made up of all co-workers! How amazing is that?! I get to do what I love and be surrounded by bff's while doing it.

I now approach life with the mantra that being myself is the only way to be and there's nothing wrong with any part of the way I'm living regardless of who understands it or doesn't. I am raising my standards to the level that those who fall below them don't even fuck with me anymore. I received beautiful, loving, respectful messages from amazing people coming out of the woodwork on my birthday last week. I also connected with some interesting people unexpectedly right after I tried out going for a meditative walk just as you had suggested for upleveling what I believe to be possible.

The biggest takeaways from this masterpiece for me are shifts in mindset, especially the part involving raising standards and not settling for crumbs because I used to love doing that. And it's just not cute anymore! Let's be honest, it never was!! But now I'm willing to do something about it by not even playing the game anymore. I can't wait to see what comes next!

Celeste

* * *

Where I Was At The Beginning: Very disenchanted with my work and business as a Makeup Artist because all I could see around me was the same boring material surfacing with the beauty community: Influencers doing another product review or turning their channel into a dramatic "reality show" or a pretty high-schooler posting selfies, claiming to be a professional and having the same glam room everyone else does. You know what I'm talking about-the silver, white and marble scheme with a cliche "Live, Laugh, Love" quote on a canvas hanging up somewhere. Needless to say, I was bitter. Everything felt so robotic and clone-like and I didn't want to be associated with that. I would constantly think "Is this all there is?"

Where I Am Now: Not even competing on the same playing field. I purchased a piece of property where I am building the world's first makeup studio (and building in general) shaped like an actual lipstick tube! How much dreamier can it get? Shopping and getting a makeup application inside a beautiful piece of novelty architecture, and walking away with souvenir lipsticks shaped like the building to remember this unforgettable experience. I've daydreamed my fantasies into existence!

THANK YOU SO MUCH!

Erin Hendley

* * *

I've been doing Magical Morning Practices with a bunch of babes for months and months, but I've realized I'm kind of going round in circles, just skating over the surface and not specifically addressing the deep issues. This is of course because I live in New Zealand and we all are very closely connected (two degrees of separation) and I didn't feel comfortable sharing the personal family stuff. So this morning I sent them a message saying I was going to keep my voice memos private for a while and not share them. Then I recorded a LONG voice memo to myself (haha when I talk to myself my cute cute accent is so strong!) Part of it was 'today I talked to [person] about [issue]'. I then started listening back and within about 20 seconds I had to stop as [person] had phoned me to talk about [issue]. The conversation went really well! I cannot believe how fast that happened once I took myself to a place of unselfconscious truth. I was like YAY YES I AM A WITCH hehe. (Lols but also I actually am) Thank you Gala you beautiful fierce guiding angel I LOVE YOU.

Nadine Armiger

* * *

My life changed in baby steps as each chapter went on. I started attracting better men, my house was starting to feel like a home, I meditated everyday but the biggest life changing moment was within the secondary benefits chapter and what story do I keep reliving found at my very core. My father sexually abused me every night for years. He used to enter my room at night when everyone was quiet and everyone was sleeping. Although, today I am a strong and independent woman, part of me still feels that paralyzing fear of those nights and when I try to take two steps ahead I keep sabotaging myself by overeating, procrastinating or isolating myself into victim mode. I decided to change the story. I did a meditation where I went back and visualized that little girl in the bed and today's version of me was standing at the edge next to the bookcase. I watched as she stared at the ceiling listening for the footsteps approaching, the creaking sounds getting louder as he walked down each step. I entered her fearful mind and told her you have a voice, you have the power to say no. This is about him trying to take control over his shame, not about you being lesser than. It's time to take back your power and as I heard the hand on the doorknob turn, the now version of me slammed a book on the floor. The steps paused, he turned around and slowly walked away. For the first time in my life, I feel that I took the final bow.

Stephanie

* * *

I've been following your blog since 2007 and you've been helping me change my perspective and attitude for so many years now! It's been such a pleasure to watch you and your business grow and evolve and honestly I am so proud of you!

Your first book was such a godsend and milestone in my self love journey so of course I was psyched when you announced Magnetic Mindset and immediately hopped on board. And hooooo boy howdy I was not expecting it to change my life so, well, radically!

Over the past 9 months, I've had so many shifts. I realized the relationship I was in was toxic and no longer serving either of us. I took the plunge and decided to love my partner from a distance. Singledom has been amazing!

Now I have the partner of my dreams in a wonderful open relationship that gives me the freedom to be my biggest, baddest self.

I also let go of some hustles that were ultimately bringing me down, and while I'm still working out the next step financially, I have found my love and passion for fiber arts. It feels so amazing to be creating again instead of just grinding away for a meager paycheck. The creative juices just keep flowing! I have so many projects and ideas on the horizon and I finally feel like I can make them a reality.

But mostly importantly, I've really stepped into my own and started living authentically as myself. This happened in a way I never expected.

I had known for a long time that the gender I was assigned didn't fit me. But doing all this work on loving and accepting myself and manifesting the life of my dreams gave me the courage—and to be quite honest, the kick in the ass—I needed to finally accept this truth.

I know so much of your work centers on empowering women, but it empowered me to realize I'm not a woman. I am a proud trans man!

Once I was able to admit that to myself, I found myself inside the vortex constantly! I shed all these expectations and bullshit narratives about what I should be and how my life should look. You made me realize I can build my identity and my life to look however I please.

Of course transitioning is a process and it isn't necessarily easy. But it is so worth it. I have been humbled and amazed by the amount of love and support I've gotten from the people in my life. Now I feel so secure in being able to realize those that don't—well, the Universe knew they weren't meant to be close to me anyway. Their issues with it are not my personal problem and that is so freeing!

So, thank you Gala. Your work is amazing and important. You really have helped me transform my life and mindset. I am happy to say that I am now living my truth and my fantasy! Life in the vortex is so fucking delicious! While it's still a work in progress, staying more consistently high vibe feels fucking fantastic and has opened up so many possibilities and opportunities for me! I'm so excited for what the Universe has in store for me!

V

Sweet, sweet Gala,

Where do I even start?! Life before Magnetic Mindset was good. But just good. I was going to school working on a double major, working full-time overnights to support myself, and traveling whenever possible. However, I was not feeling myself fully. I had discarded my spiritual practice of tarot, visualization, and gratitude in exchange for complaining, reliving old trauma by choosing the same old people and places, and saying 'no' to the things I should have been saying 'yes' to, and vice versa.

My best friend introduced me to you, honestly. She asked if she could send me her magical mornings and that I would be welcome to join in, but didn't have to. I happily listened to her for a couple of weeks and it just made me feel good. I had put off sending my own recordings in return and then I was just finally sick of making excuses why I wouldn't. As soon as I decided to jump in, everything started to change. Slowly, but there was change.

One month in, I realized that I really need to start addressing my own truth and tell my story for the first time in my entire life. I had victimized myself for decades, even when I thought I wasn't doing it anymore. And finally I said, "Fuck it!" and gave myself permission to be involved in a community rather than insisting that no one else had my problems. After writing out a short story of my life, I shared it with my closest people and felt a full release of the old self so I could start vibing fucking higher! Shortly after that, I gave myself permission to focus on my work as an artist and began producing art at a rapid speed. I also encouraged myself to apply to a highly sought after academic program, the best in the world for its field, and see what would happen. After I sent that in, I just let the rest flow. I went to Spain and Portugal for six weeks with my best friend where every morning we did our ritual practice together, creating space and high energy for the other's dreams and new lives. It was all we did and talked about while we explored beautiful terrain and plotted our new deserving selves.

Coming back from that magical space being with one of the most amazing humans to ever exist, I realized it was time to let go of all the energy leaks in my life. If they couldn't get on this new glittery Lamborghini I was cruisin' through the hills on, then it was time to keep rolling. I ended friendships that had long overstayed their welcome, I quit my overnight job that I had let rob me of my sleep for three years, and ended leaks with lovers who were not able to show up for their own selves first. Once I finally made that choice, everything began moving at an exponential rate.

I began having galleries in the center of the metropolitan city in which I reside make space for my art. National awards, publications, and recognitions were coming my way not only for my sculptural work, but my literary, as well. I met an amazing and kind lover who seeks to live their own joy. I started a business with my best friend/cofounder, and was accepted into the international academic program of choice (just one of 40 accepted!).

So much magic has happened. However, the most marvelous thing about all of this is that I have been made more aware of my own truth and that I fucking DESERVE to have all the beauty and love because there is an infinite supply. And having a community has been such a crucial aspect of this whole experience because I insisted that I was alone for so long.

Had I not had this newfound and solidified awareness, I would have never been able to get through one of the most life-altering moments of my life. Back in April, I was told by my doctors that I had an abnormal mass in my brain. To keep the story short, six weeks later it was completely gone. Every day I meditated and visualized my life how I knew it was possible to be with all of the love and community that I desired and deserved. I utilized float tanks every day, spoke out my gratitude for the abundance of my life, and had an intensity of living in the present moment (because I was actually wanting to now) that completely transformed me.

I have always believed in magic. But now I actually live that magic. And girl, I'm telling you, without the community that you have fostered and encouraged, I honestly don't think I would be where I am now, or where I'm going, without it.

Here's to raising the fucking standard. *raises a Perrier lime*

Thank you. You sweet, wild woman!

Vana Black

* * *

I want to share with you how this book and practice has transformed my life. First, let me just say THANK YOU!!! THANK YOU!! THANK YOU!! You've absolutely changed my life 100% for the better.

I started Magnetic Mindset on my birthday. It felt symbolic. I had a gut feeling it was going to be major but I had no idea just how major it would be.

The Universe knew I needed some serious help pushing me to level up in every way so I was gifted not one, but three beautiful, inspiring, kind partners. Each one offers a unique perspective. These women have not only listened to me be vulnerable, they've also celebrated all of my victories. With their constant support I've been able to make some massive changes in my life.

I was able to close the door on a 13 year relationship that was over but we were living in the same home raising our daughter. Although it was a temporary solution we were both lingering and holding onto the comfort of the past. We are currently navigating raising our daughter as communicative co-parents and building a beautiful friendship.

I now live in my dream condo that is more than I could have ever imagined, including a master bathroom with a jetted tub and a glass shower and double sinks for all my glam and a killer closet. It's in the best neighborhood and is just a five minutes drive to my two best friends' homes.

I have also landed my dream job which fell into my lap. It has provided me with some amazing opportunities for growth in my career and gives me the stability to afford my beautiful home and life comfortably and best of all, I get to live my passion daily which feeds my soul and makes me so wildly happy.

This daily morning practice and working through the chapters in the book with the support of your tapping videos has been the most life changing experience. I now trust the Universe to always have my back. I look at rejection as redirection. And live the mantra this or something better.

I have never been more excited for what's in store for my future but at the same time fully living and loving my current life and the journey.

I am so GRATEFUL for you and the gift you've given me and all these women.

Alicia Roy

✳ ✳ ✳

It was October 2018. Courtney Pearce, Virtual Assistant and creator of the VA training program VA Vixen, was surrounded by negative people. She felt lost and untethered -to herself, to community, to her purpose. She knew that she needed to change her life. She sent text messages to a few of the most toxic people in her life saying that she needed to take a break to focus on herself and that same day she signed up for Magnetic Mindset. On the other side of the country in Hawaii, Kimi Morton, Business Coach and co-founder of Boss Up Media, was feeling overworked, tired, and frustrated. Her businesses were just not creating the abundance or fulfillment that she craved. She knew she was playing small and not fully expressing herself. In her pursuit of something to shift her energy, she signed up for Magnetic Mindset.

Neither Courtney or Kimi knew what was in store for them. They literally just thought they were going to be reading a book. Instead, they got access to the infamous google sheet that changed their lives forever. Following instructions to pick a Magical Morning partner from this list of Magnetic Mindset participants, Kimi saw Courtney's name and everything her soul just KNEW that she had to reach out to Courtney from North Carolina immediately. From that day forward they committed themselves to daily Magical Morning voice memos to each other. 263 days straight as of June 2019 and they are still going!

From the beginning, the practice was powerful for both of them.

They very quickly began to see and feel tangible results in their lives. Courtney created the online course she had been dreaming of for years with ease and joy. Kimi and her business partner made a radical pivot and rebranded their coaching/digital media business to become the business of their dreams. Even though life wasn't perfect, every day, they expanded, trading negative energy for positive, as they committed to making FEELING GOOD their number one job. They even did monthly zoom calls after reading each chapter of the book to reflect, celebrate, and set intentions for the month ahead.

But the practice became even more meaningful and important when Courtney got very ill in December 2018. Voice memos became Courtney's prayers and the girls held each other strong through a rough few months of navigating pain, fear, and the unknown. In February 2019, Court was officially diagnosed with head and neck cancer. Although it would have been easy to put the Magical Morning Practice on hold, Courtney and Kimi dove deeper into the practice and devoted themselves even more to each other's visions.

The next three months were very intense. Courtney and her loving boyfriend Tyler packed up and moved to be closer to Levine Cancer Institute to start the grueling process of cancer treatment which included three surgeries and countless scans, tests, and doctors' visits. Throughout all of this, there wasn't a single day that the girls missed their voice memo practice. Even when Courtney couldn't speak because of her mouth surgery, her boyfriend Tyler stepped up and did Courtney's voice memo for her, channeling her vision and bringing much-needed humor to a dark day.

The doctors were certain that Courtney would need chemotherapy and radiation to clear the cancer, but Court and Kimi held strong to their vision of her not needing anything more than surgery. Every day they visualized themselves in Hawaii celebrating her being healthy, happy, and cancer-free. And then, just three months after her diagnosis, Courtney blew the minds of her doctors and everyone around her when was declared cancer-free on May 22, 2019.

After many tearful voice memos full of gratitude and amazement, they began to visualize how Courtney would celebrate this new chapter of her life and how they could honor the beautiful sisterhood they shared, the sisterhood that carried them through such a challenging time. They knew they needed to meet in real life, they had seen it in their visions almost every day. Then, Gala Darling, their magical Magnetic Mindset fairy godmother gifted Courtney with the abundance to buy a ticket to Hawaii. Before they knew it they were hugging in person and crying tears of gratitude for this ultimate manifestation. Their story is now inspiring others to start their own Magical Morning Practices and, most importantly, to believe that ANYTHING IS POSSIBLE!!!!!!!!!!!

This is just the beginning for Courtney and Kimi. After mind-blowing adventures in Hawaii together, they are now stepping into even greater versions of themselves and expanding their vision even more. They want to inspire others to dream bigger, believe in miracles, CHOOSE to feel good every day, and open their hearts to receive. They credit Magnetic Mindset and the Magical Morning Practice for helping them to tap into more resilience, power, and magic than they could have ever imagined.

WE FUCKING LOVE YOU!!!!!!!

Courtney Pearce and Kimi Morton

WHEN I STARTED WRITING THIS BOOK, IT WAS WITH the knowledge that we are all capable of changing our lives and creating any permutation of a delicious life that we desire. I believed that desire was healthy and normal; that we are required to honor our desires; that moving towards what we wanted would broaden our lives; and that digging deep into the utter joy of every moment was the purpose of being alive. I wanted to share those beliefs with you, show you examples from my own life that would inspire you to keep pushing through, especially when things felt uncertain, and provide you with practical exercises that would move your life forward in a fun and exciting way.

As much as my own life has been transformed with the creation of this book, it pales in comparison to the incredible strides made by those of you who have been reading. For so many of you, life looked completely different. Many of you have moved homes and even countries; changed or massively improved your relationships; overthrown the way you make money; and taken on health challenges with the grit, faith, and fierceness of warrior queens.

Your life may look different to the casual observer, but what has happened on the inside of you is even more impressive.

Your thinking is bigger and more expansive. Gratitude is a daily cornerstone of your life. You trust that the Universe is supporting you. You see the beauty in ordinary things. And you see the beauty in yourself.

It gives me goosebumps to think about it. Pride and joy swells in my heart.

It is one thing to shift your own life, and it is entirely another to see the ripples as everyone around you does the same. I am deeply inspired by these stories: by the friendship, the courage, the vulnerability and the commitment to self.

These testimonials prove to me, beyond a shadow of a doubt, that you can change absolutely anything in your life. The benevolence of the Universe is available to all of us. We are surrounded by infinite love and eternal possibility.

Our biggest challenge is simply to trust that the Universe is there for us, that we will be cared and provided for. As you can see from this chapter, there are examples of this all around us, at all times. Sometimes we don't notice it. Sometimes we get bogged down and we feel stuck. But when we truly commit to ourselves, the Universe will always rise up to meet us. It will hold our hands and gently nudge us towards what feels good. As long as we keep listening, we will always be surrounded by love, miracles and deep joy.

Always, Gala

ISBN: 979-8-218-03056-8

Front and back cover images: Madeline Northway. madelinenorthway.com
Book design and layout: We Are Branch. wearebranch.com
Photo retouching: Bianca Alexis. biancaalexis.com

First printing edition, 2022.

Gala Darling
⌨ galadarling.com
◎ @galadarling